LONDON TRANSPORT

BUSES & COACHES

1957

LONDON TRANSPORT
BUSES & COACHES

1957

Including a supplement of
photographs covering the years
1953-56

John A.S. Hambley

Published in 1999 by
JOHN A.S. HAMBLEY
7 Linden Road,
Dunstable,
Beds. LU5 4NZ

Additional text and research by David A. Ruddom

British Library Cataloguing in Publication Data
A catalogue record for this book is available from the British Library

ISBN 0 9533146 2 6

Designed and produced by Hedgehog.
Printed and bound in Great Britain.

All overhauled buses and coaches were returned to service with a silver paint finish to their chassis and running units and this is clearly visible in this picture of RT2273 just four days into service following its visit to Aldenham in April. It waits departure from Victoria Station on a quiet looking Saturday 4th May for a journey to Potters Bar Station by way of Route 134 with other RTs in use on Routes 38 and 16 in the background. (W.R.Legg)

In a grey and dark red livery with the added convenience of platform doors, ex-Craven RT1518 is seen at West Row, Mildenhall while in the ownership of Morley's Coaches who traded as Grey's Coaches. The date is 8th September, less than twelve months since its purchase but overhanging tree branches in the Suffolk countryside have caused front dome damage while paint already seems to be parting company with the glass of the side blind box. (A.R.Packer)

Acknowledgements

Once again it gives me great pleasure to thank everyone who has helped in one way or another to bring to fruition this latest volume in the series of books looking at London Transport buses and coaches through the years. Without the kind co-operation, understanding and wealth of knowledge willingly shared by so many transport enthusiasts the content would be the poorer.

To those who have allowed me to use their photographic work or collections in this new volume a special thank you. These include: James H.Aston, Colin Bull, C.Carter, Frank Church, Alan B.Cross, Alistair J.Douglas, Michael Dryhurst, John Gascoine, J.C.Gillham, Peter Gulland, Roy Hobbs, F.W.Ivey, D.A.Jones, D.W.K.Jones, D.P.Kirker, Kevin Lane, Alan Mortimer, National Tramway Museum, A.G.Newman, Tony R.Packer, 'Photobus', the late J.H.Price, Norman Rayfield, Michael Rooum, Lyndon Rowe, David A.Ruddom, R.H.G.Simpson, John G.S.Smith, P.J.Snell, R.E.Stevens, Sheila Taylor of the London Transport Museum, Ron Wellings, J.Wills and A.M.Wright.

As usual the publications produced by The London Historical Research Group of the Omnibus Society, The London Omnibus Traction Society, The PSV Circle and The RT/RF Register have been of invaluable help in compiling the text for this volume. Thanks are extended accordingly and interested readers are encouraged to join and support these societies.

I should particularly like to thank David Ruddom for the considerable time and energy he has spent in assisting me with suggestions, text and in preparing the final manuscript for printing. My wife Iris and David's wife Enid are also thanked for the continued patience and understanding they show to two very keen bus enthusiasts.

Publisher's Note

As with all my publications, photographs not credited or credited to other people's collections have been accepted lacking any identification as to their origin. If thereby credit to any photographer has been inadvertently omitted, I apologise sincerely and would ask that they contact me so that the omission can be rectified in future volumes. Kevin Lane has been involved with the printing of many of the photographs used in this book and if you have a negative that lacks a decent print he can be contacted at 15 Beech Green, Dunstable, Beds LU6 1EB. Please continue to dig out those older negatives from wherever they have lain for so many years. It may be that it is the gem that other enthusiasts and historians have been searching for. Although I have now published books covering all the years from 1939 to 1957 and 1961/62, it is still possible to include pictures from these years in supplements in later volumes and a selection of interesting shots that have recently come to hand from the 1950s are included at the end of this volume.

Introduction

The year started with the effect of fuel rationing resulting from the Suez crisis in full swing. Cuts were made in services outside the rush hours, chiefly in the evenings and at weekends although the special revisions to the timetables which were issued stated that the alterations would not apply at Bank Holidays. There was of course a certain irony in the situation in that the general public were more desirous of using public transport because of the impact on the use of private cars, which was just beginning to gain momentum.

A gradual return to normal passenger service commenced on 1st April when the first rationing measures were lifted and then on the 14th May the restrictions were finally withdrawn allowing the Private Hire and Tours Department the freedom to introduce a programme of tours and excursions at the beginning of June. There was also a large programme of special services to major sporting events, which reflects the far greater reliance on public transport evident in 1957 compared to today.

In general the number of changes to routes made throughout the year were rather more abundant than in the previous year. Introduction of routes included the 98B, 179A, 193, 198, 199, 224B, 263 in the Central Area and quite a few in the Country Area many of which were variations of routes to provide works and school services. The pattern of localising main trunk routes continued and 49, 74, 77A, 113, 133 and 134 were among those so treated in the year under review.

Despite the effects of the fuel crisis and all this re-vamping of services the peak of service provision had already passed and this is reflected in the total number of passenger carrying vehicles owned. During the years 1950 through to and including 1955 the total vehicle stock figure was in five figures but by the end of 1957 this had dropped to 9478. This declining trend was to continue thereafter year in and year out with just the occasional 'blip' although it has to be admitted that in modern times, with so many operators and such a fragmented situation, it is difficult to make accurate comparisons.

One big event during the year was the introduction of the Central Area 5/- Rover Ticket at weekends. This followed the success of the Country Area equivalent. In essence, apart from the pre-war 1/- all day tram tickets, this was the first time anything approaching the modern day Travelcard had been made available.

A new West London Air Terminal, built over the famous 'Cromwell Curve' on the District Line, was opened to traffic on 6th October, the previous site at the South Bank, Waterloo being required for redevelopment. Unfortunately the new site was rather inconvenient to reach to say the least. In consequence the BEA fleet of coaches were moved from their basement garage at Gillingham Street, Victoria to Shepherds Bush garage.

The only new vehicles delivered during the year were the remaining two prototype Routemasters. RML3 (the 'L' denoting the Leyland engine with which it was fitted rather than lengthened) was to be the only Weymann bodied example within the class and CRL4 was the unique ECW bodied coach version which, in terms of passenger service, was the longest lived of the prototypes.

The AEC Monocoach NLP635 was returned to its owners on 1st May while on 31st August the last of the pre-war fleet in the shape of the 2RTs were withdrawn from service. Disposals during the year amounted to forty one buses made up of the residue of the Craven bodied RTs which totalled 24; a further sixteen of the AEC T class (fifteen pre-war and one post-war example) and one STL, leaving fourteen remaining of that once vast class.

Tours abroad by London Transport buses during the year were relatively few. RT2422 left for a 'British Week' event in Leeuwarden, Holland, being away from 15th June to 7th August. The same bus accompanied by RTL1486 later visited Helsinki, Finland to attend a trade fair held between 6th and 22nd September. Both vehicles quickly returned to normal duties after arriving back in England.

During the year London Transport's bus workers formulated 'a substantial wage claim' which was submitted for consideration by the Transport and General Workers' Union. This was to lead to events, which would radically reshape London Transport bus and coach services but that is next year's story.

Airport coach MLL722, having made a connection with a Guernsey flight, is seen waiting outside the original London Heathrow Airport terminal which is now known as Terminal 2. In total sixty five of this style of coach, owned by British European Airways but operated by London Transport, entered service, being identified by their registration numbers although given the L.T. classification 4RF4. October saw the opening of the Gloucester Road, West London Air Terminal situated above the Cromwell Curve on the District Line and the Waterloo site was vacated for eventual office development. With the introduction of the Airbus services and hotel routes; the extension of the Piccadilly Line and the Heathrow Express from Paddington, the use of such vehicles as the 4RF4s would be rather inadequate in today's situation.

Chelverton Road garaged RTL1102 is seen at the Wandsworth terminus of Route 28 on the 6th May with RTL69, a Middle Row resident, parked further along the road. Just under 14 years service in the capital was achieved by the higher numbered bus and after its second visit to Aldenham in October 1958 it spent its last few years in passenger use operating from Victoria garage. (W.R.Legg)

Unlike the other Country Area liveried 15T13 shown elsewhere in this book on Central Area duties, T773 never returned to its rightful sphere of operations but was placed in store at London Road, Romford garage to gather dust for over a year before eventually being disposed of. Hampton Court had lost its day trippers and tourists by the time this 22nd November picture was taken as the bus approaches the station with the elegant bridge across the Thames in the background which had been opened in 1933. (J.C.Gillham)

Looking resplendent after its July visit to Aldenham for overhaul, RT4704 is captured on film at Crystal Palace on 12th October. With its destination blind reset for a return journey to Shepherds Bush Green by the Merton garage driver, all that is now required are a few passengers to make use of the service, which is a pity since the two gentlemen lurking in the car hire office doorway look very much like loading inspectors. (W.R.Legg)

Route 79A took to the roads of the capital on 6th August 1952 operating between Edgware Station and Perivale with a peak hour extension to Northolt Airport. By 1957 the Northolt extension had been cut back to The Target public house. RT1829 waits for departure at the 'Weekday Rush Hours Only' bus stop on Western Avenue at Northolt. This must therefore be the 'rush hour', but where is the rush hour traffic? Present day A40 commuters will find this picture hard to believe. (Ron Wellings)

Palmers Green's RT376 at Victoria works the Sunday through service on Route 29 to South Mimms. It carries one of the original via point blinds designed for the Southgate to Victoria weekday working. These early examples of full blind displays had some idiosyncrasies and this is a good example. Why the compilers chose to include Holloway Road is a mystery, since the route only crossed this thoroughfare. Seven Sisters Road or Camden Road might have been rather more appropriate. (W.R.Legg)

Standing in the Crawley garage yard, RT4475 displays route blinds for the limited stop service 851 which operated on Sunday afternoons between Three Bridges railway station and the Smallfield Hospital. This southern area eight hundred series route first took to the roads on 30th May 1954, eventually to be withdrawn after operation on 26th September 1965 when it was replaced by a revision to the 482 route which also served the hospital. The bus, despite wearing Country Area livery, had first entered service from Twickenham garage in March 1954. Four years later, after having been used at Addlestone, Crawley and Garston, it received an overhaul to be outshopped in Central Area colours, which it carried until eventually disposed of in August 1970. (A.R.Packer)

Two lowbridge buses are seen parked at the Woodcote garage premises of Chiltern Queens on 28th July. Ex-STL1959 in the foreground had an interesting history in that the chassis carrying a highbridge LPTB body numbered 17231 first entered service in June 1937. It received an overhaul in March 1939 re-entering service carrying an identical body numbered 17289. This body was transferred to the float system at Chiswick in January 1943 and the chassis reappeared with one of the twenty new lowbridge bodies built at Chiswick Works - this one numbered 464. Disposed of in December 1952 it had seen service with Hants & Dorset before acquisition by Kemp's Motor Services Ltd. of Woodcote and eventual purchase by Chiltern Queens in July 1955. Withdrawn in 1958 it lingered on deteriorating until finally scrapped at Woodcote in March 1960. JWL731 beyond was a Guy Arab originally in the fleet of City of Oxford. (J.C.Gillham)

Ex-T594 had in September 1942 been sent to the O.C. Motor Base of the US Forces in England, Ashchurch, Gloucestershire for use by the US Army for the duration of the war. One of a large group of 10T10s to move to Ashchurch, this particular vehicle was one of a number not returned after the hostilities had ended and its history is surrounded by intrigue. It was amazingly identified in March 1946, re-registered and in the ownership of the Reading operator Smith's Luxury Coaches. How this happened has never been established. Someone recently suggested that a role model for Sgt.Bilko might have been involved! That is as may be but after passing through the hands of Kemp of Woodcote it finally ended its days with Chiltern Queens of Woodcote from July 1955 until scrapped in August 1960. Seen in a red and cream livery on 2nd June it is parked at the Woodcote garage yard not being withdrawn from passenger use until August 1958. (A.R.Packer)

STL827 existed between July 1935, when it first entered service at Dalston garage, and April 1960 when scrapped by W.North, the well known dealer. After its many years of passenger use with London Transport, which finished at Upton Park when it became the very last pre-war STL in service on 29th June 1954, it was to languish unlicensed for a period at the old Forest Road works, Walthamstow. It then went to J.W.Lloyd & Sons Ltd. of Oswestry as their fleet number 6 between September 1955 until in March 1960 it was withdrawn and returned to the dealer who first handled its sale. The recognisable livery of the STL11 type LPTB built bodywork confirms that only a partial repaint had been afforded the machine when photographed on 5th September. (V.C.Jones)

The Salvation Army hall on the western side of Hertford Bus Station was a familiar background to Green Line pictures for many years. RF77, a Guildford garaged coach lays over on Route 715 on 26th March before returning to its home town. At one time coaches shuttled back to Hertford garage for the lay over but this does not seem to be the case here. The RF class were superseded with double deck RMCs from 29th August 1962 onwards, albeit with a drop in frequency from 20 to 30 minutes. (W.R.Legg)

The lengthwise advertisement carried by RT1168 confirms that in 1957 £75,000 had been paid for a 2d (not quite 5p) stake by Vernons Pools and shows the popularity of this form of gamble in pre-lottery days. The date is 5th August and it is interesting to note the increasing size of the the top prize when this picture is compared to other Football Pools advertisements carried by buses in earlier volumes of this series of books. Route number 57, last used in November 1942, was resurrected with the demise of the trams in the capital, being used with the second stage of the conversion programme on 7th January 1951. Brixton garage had been involved in the operation from the beginning and this was to last until 1964 when the route lost its Victoria section and received a long extension south west to Kingston. (W.R.Legg)

On 28th August RT2422 is already being made secure while RTL1486 is still in the process of being lifted into place for the journey to Finland as deck cargo. This was to be the second tour abroad made by London buses during the year under review. Both buses had been prepared at Reigate garage for their British Trade Fair experience in Helsinki, not arriving back in England until the early days of October. From this angle a clear view is obtained of the differences in roof panelling of the two buses. Finnish wording is carried on the AEC advertisements, presumably a Leyland version has been late in arriving for the front nearside of the RTL. (L.T.Museum 141718)

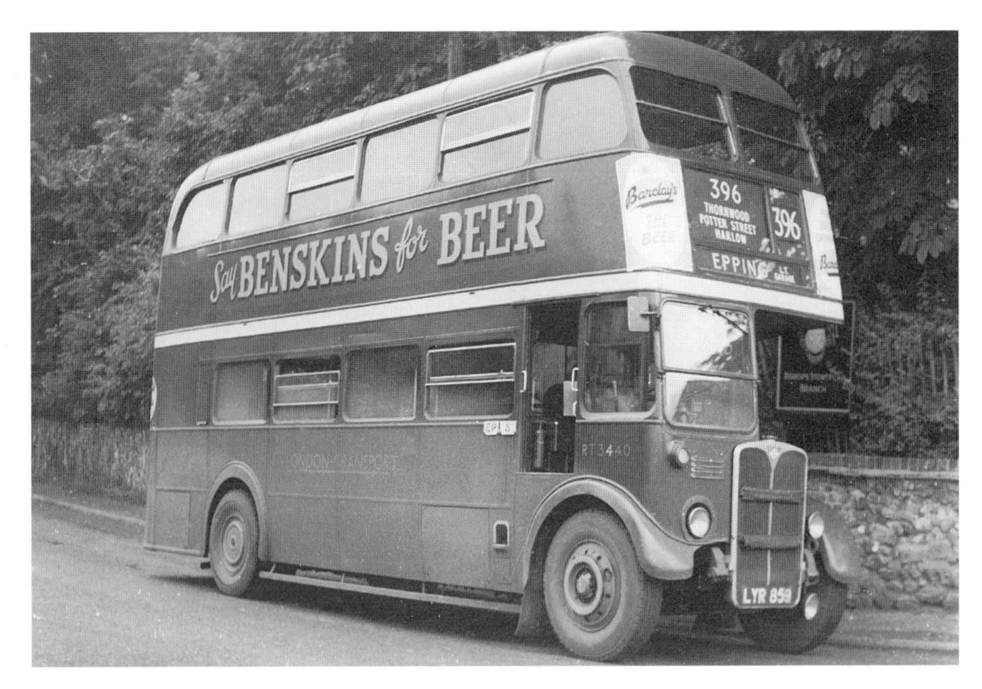

First entering service with London Transport at Epping garage in February 1952 and scrapped by the Wombwell Diesels Company in October 1976, RT3440 just missed out by around eight months on reaching its silver jubilee celebrations, which would have matched the Queen's exactly. Having re-entered service at Epping after receiving an initial overhaul in October 1955, it is now seen at the Bishops Stortford terminus of Route 396 at a time when it would appear that intermediate point blinds were in short supply. Route 396 was born out of the wartime withdrawal of Green Line services and while the main service used the trunk A11 road between Epping and Bishops Stortford, there were many ancillary workings which ventured into the labyrinthine roads of Harlow New Town.

Kingsbury Square in the market town of Aylesbury looks most tranquil with a background steeped in history. RLH42, together with various 20th century roadside additions brings it all up to the present day. After a short sojourn at Harrow Weald garage upon its re-entry into service after overhaul in July 1956, this bus, which always carried green livery, found itself in use for the first time at Amersham where it was to spend the rest of its passenger carrying years. It was disposed of in March 1965 and subsequently became a mobile furniture showroom. (R.Wellings)

GS8 is seen at Edenbridge while on service 485 with route blind set for a journey to Westerham via Crockham Hill. The route had been converted to GS operation with the first mass entry into service of these one-man operated buses in November 1953. This example had first been allocated to Hitchin and entered service at Chelsham following its first overhaul. Except for the painted radiator surround it looks almost as if it was a brand new bus. (C.Carter)

Chestnut paling fencing is rarely seen nowadays but here it edges the road at the Mitcham terminus of Route 152. On 26th February RT4608 is working one of the three duty schedules on the route allocated to Kingston garage on Monday to Friday. Earlier in the month the bus had re-entered service after its first overhaul. Prior to this event it had been a resident of Merton since new and therefore its presence on Route 152 was not unfamiliar. (W.R.Legg)

RFW14, having brought a party to the Ascot Races on 22nd June is parked on the grass until the return journey later in the day. It is surrounded by contemporary examples of the coaching scene rather different to the AEC Regal Mark IV chassis and ECW 39 seat bodywork of the RFW. It is one of only two of this small class known to survive in the preservation movement, the other being RFW6.
(A.R.Packer)

RT816 journeys to Norwood Junction in and out of the shadows cast by the buildings in George Street, Croydon while in use on Route 197. Though fitted with a roof box type body, this was replaced in December 1959 upon the vehicle's third overhaul, which helped ensure longevity for the fleet number. It was not despatched for scrap until 1979, the last year of passenger operation of the RT class in London. (A.Mortimer)

RT1173 stands in the Victoria Station forecourt with destination blind set for the peak hour working to Hornchurch Station. Until May 1950 this trunk section of the 25 group of routes had been numbered 25B while the plain 25 number only appeared on Sundays between Stratford and Little Heath. A sensible rationalisation gave the basic number to the main route. Forest Gate garage had been allocated this Park Royal bodied bus since its return to service from overhaul in May. Originally a Saunders manufactured body, number 2452, had graced the chassis when it entered service at Elmers End garage in May 1949. After a subsequent spell at Rye Lane, April 1963 saw the early disposal of this bus. (A.R.Packer)

H.Brown, who traded as Garelochead Coach Services, acquired Craven bodied RT1427 in July 1956 and it saw passenger service with this operator through to March 1960. On acquisition the London Transport blind display was reduced to just the destination box and the bus was repainted into its new operator's colours. Further use was assured for the bus when it was sold on to Hill & Paterson of Stevenston, consortium members of the Ayrshire Bus Owners' A1 Services. The vehicle's Scottish connection was finally ended in July 1963 when it was scrapped by a dealer named Smith who had premises in Glasgow.

The chassis of ex-STL744 provided the basis for a furniture van of considerable proportions and was used from 1955 through to July 1958 by Exeloak Ltd. of Tottenham, N17. First entering service in April 1935 with an LPTB body seating 56 passengers, it was to serve Londoners until withdrawn in April 1954. Some four months later it found itself at the Lancashire Motor Traders' premises at Salford who prepared the chassis for its new role and despatched it to J.S.Kean of Hackney, E9 for building its new body. It is seen in a rather worn and grubby state with a Humber car on the right of the picture and a Hillman Minx just visible to the left.

It was still another seven years before the 122 route would be extended across south east London to become a major trunk route and in 1957 it still just ran between Woolwich and Bexleyheath Trolleybus Depot. Plumstead's RT2304 is the third of seven vehicles allocated to the service on Sunday 3rd March and heads east at the start of its journey from Woolwich. (W.R.Legg)

Resting after its long haul on excursion duties from Reigate garage, Green Line liveried RF289 stands beside the navigational waters of the River Wensum at Norwich. The occasion, towards the end of the year, was when 'minnows' Redhill F.C. were drawn against Norwich City in the F.A.Cup. The vehicle had originally entered service in September 1952 as the first Central Area RF with seating for 41 passengers. It was repainted into Green Line colours, fitted with saloon doors and luggage racks for its new role in March 1956, having its seating reduced to 40 some months later. (R.Hobbs)

Route number 163 had been resurrected on 6th July 1952 having lain dormant since its previous use for a Sunday service between Wormwood Scrubs and Becontree Heath which ceased in February 1949. With the final stage of the tram conversion programme the number was used for a service between Plumstead Common and Westminster, Horse Guards Avenue replacing Tram 40 and using STL, RT and RTL buses. New Cross garaged RT852 waits departure from Plumstead Common for a run to the Embankment on 31st August. It was RT852 which caused a stir when new, being the first non-roof box red RT. Ironically it now carries a body that has one. (W.R.Legg)

From January through to December of the year under review, T770 was in use as a staff bus garaged at Reigate. It is seen here at Reigate returning to its home from some sort of duty on Derby day. In the following year this Mann Egerton bodied bus dating from March 1948 was exported to Ceylon. (R.Hobbs)

Former RT1475 embellished with an AEC triangle on its radiator but lacking its roof box is now number 1 in the fleet of Red Rover of Aylesbury. Seen on 28th July at Kingsbury Square within its home town, it has already attracted an acceptable level of patronage. Eventually it will depart on the seven mile journey to Westcott serving the Haydon Hill suburb of Aylesbury and then using mainly the A41 trunk road. (J.C.Gillham)

Green liveried RT36 waits for further use on Route 327 at a deserted Hertford bus station on 26th March. Later in the year under review post-war RTs replaced the Hertford garaged 2RT2 type buses and their seventeen-year term of passenger use in London came to an end on 31st August. (W.R.Legg)

RT428 operates from Norbiton garage in its last full year of service with London Transport before disposal to Bird's of Stratford-upon-Avon in July of the following year. TD107, also garaged at Norbiton, departed the fleet in March 1960 for the far more exotic destination of Ceylon. The location is the Kingston railway station terminus on a Sunday in the early part of the year. After 1st May Norbiton lost its Sunday only allocation of three vehicles on the 216 route. (A.R.Packer)

The Derby race day in the year under review saw the Reigate garage trainer bus RT111 parked at Tattenham Corner for the day as a control point of sorts. Other London Transport vehicles in use on excursion duties to the Downs include an RF having journeyed from Garston, a Watford High Street RT with a further example beyond. The queue of intending passengers wait patiently for a bus on the section of Route 406 to Reigate, as on race days the route which normally traversed the Downs to reach Epsom and Kingston was split into two sections. (Roy Hobbs)

RT3195 stands within the well-illuminated interior of Grays garage on 16th February. In the far corner, beside some building materials, a Ford Thames 10cwt. van can also be seen. The bus appears to have last been used on the 380 route to Linford, which was to disappear in May 1958. Two months before that this RT would be overhauled and change to Central Area livery, effectively ending its period of operation in the Country Area which had lasted since first entry into service at High Wycombe in June 1950. (A.R.Packer)

After its withdrawal from passenger service, the chassis of T256 was used in July 1939 as the basis for service vehicle 408W. In its new capacity of a 6½ ton open lorry it continued in the ownership of London Transport until disposed of to W.North & Sons in April 1962. Carrying a heavy load of underground train wheel and axle assemblies and closely followed by a Ford Zodiac II, it passes over traffic light impulse rubbers set into the road surface. A Central Distribution Services, Chiswick, plate is in place on the side of the body. The National Provincial Bank and Pearks, the grocers, are both names, which have disappeared from our High Streets today. (J.Gascoine collection)

GS36 re-entered service at Guildford garage after its December 1956 overhaul, having previously operated at Dorking from December 1953. Here it is working route 448 at Onslow Street bus station, Guildford and the driver/conductor appears to be preparing for another journey. (M.Rooum)

Standing in the forecourt of 'The Rose' public house at St.Helier, RT850 is kept company on 17th August by a small number of cars, the most prominent being from the Ford factory. Pub forecourts were popular sites for bus terminals until the growth of car ownership meant landlords wanted the space for customer parking. This site however was developed in later years to enhance the shopping facilities at this location midway between Morden and Sutton with only the large roundabout, visible in the background, remaining intact. The bus will eventually resume service to Acton Green, which was served by the 88 route from 1914 to 1990. (W.R.Legg)

Former London vehicles STL1854 and D31 are seen in West Hartlepool during September having both reached their last full year of use. Retained for various works services in and around the steelworks and coalmines in the area, both vehicles have reached their nadir in passenger use and are now destined for scrap in the following year. The STL11 body carried by DLU221 appears unbalanced without its route roof box while the Daimler clearly shows its utility qualities in more ways than one. (R.Hobbs)

RT917 had first entered service operating from Hounslow garage in November 1948 and is seen at Edgware on 22nd February standing on the site of the present bus station while in use on Route 18 from Alperton garage. During the intervening period the RT had worked at New Cross, Hendon and Edgware garages while also visiting the main works for two overhauls. A long London future lay ahead as it achieved nearly thirty years of passenger service within the capital before being sold for scrapping to Wombwell Diesels in Yorkshire. (W.R.Legg)

The bespectacled driver of TD53 based at Hornchurch is determined to be seen in the best light before taking his bus back to Romford Station from Romford, Birch Road by way of Route 252. Originating as a Romford & District service between Birch Road and Noak Hill the route was one-man operated, surviving in this mode right up to 1949. In January 1958 the crewed single decks, as seen here, were replaced by double deck RT buses and the route extended beyond Birch Road to Collier Row, White Hart Lane. (A.Mortimer)

RT4489 through to RT4509 were added to the fleet in 1954, being additional Green Line examples but carrying bodies once mounted on modified STL chassis and numbered in the ill fated SRT class. RT4498 complete with a raised Green Line motif waits at the Minories bus and coach station at Aldgate for departure to Grays on service 723A while the trolleybuses circle round before departing to their less distant destinations.

Red liveried RT243 is seen as a Bank Holiday duplicate at Chelsham in use on Route 403 operating only between West Croydon and Westerham on 5th August. Behind is RT3169 covering rather more of the route to Sevenoaks. Just why the red bus appears to be decanting its passengers at this apparently remote spot is not certain. Upon its second visit to works for overhaul in March of the following year the green RT behind would re-enter service in red livery, while in the following month the red RT would be disposed of with its current body, number 1500. (A.G.Newman)

At the Perry Vale, Forest Hill terminus of route 124 on 3rd March RT4435 attracts patronage before departure on its next journey to Eltham, Southend Crescent. The body originally fitted to SRT23 had been carried when the bus first entered service in December 1953 operating from Sutton garage and after a short spell in use at Hounslow, its first visit to Aldenham for overhaul took place in September 1956. From this date a Park Royal built RT3 body was fitted for a time and the bus is seen here in that combination. (W.R.Legg)

RTW231 re-entered service at Putney Bridge garage after receiving its second overhaul in April of the year under review. Previously it had been used in passenger service at Edgware, Hackney and Riverside. The seated conductor exchanges conversation with the driver standing on the platform before embarking on a journey from the Empress Hall at West Brompton to Camden Town as F16 on Route 74. The advertisements carried have stayed the course of time and are still likely to be found on London buses to this day. (A.Mortimer)

Route 157 originated in 1926 as one of the feeder services to the newly opened Northern Line Morden extension and ran from there down to Wallington. A northward projection to Raynes Park came in 1935. Working the route on 17th August RT1191, which originally carried a Saunders body, looks resplendent after its second overhaul carrying a Weymann example, number 8664. Nineteen months later the route was to double in length by providing half of the replacement for trolleybus 654 to Crystal Palace. (W.R.Legg)

En-route to Belmont Station at St.Helier, RT4410 displays one of the destination blinds made in 1951 which included the word 'only' for short workings. This is one of those English rarities, a warm August Bank Holiday Monday, and the shops are closed including Montague Burton the tailors. Their shop is the imposing white faced edifice on the left of the picture and this outfitter built several of this type of frontage around the country in their heyday. The chassis of the bus dates from December 1953 and it originally carried a body previously mounted on SRT59. In this view body number 1556 is now carried, previously mounted on RT307 and new in February 1948. The bus was therefore an early candidate for disposal despite the high fleet number and this occurred in April 1963. (W.R.Legg)

When one compares this picture with that of Q12 which appears in the 1949 supplement to the 1946 book of this series, the only noticeable difference is the livery of its new owners, Gilbert-Ash, and the screwed on registration plate. The vehicle is seen parked at the old Gatwick Airport near the Beehive terminal building, which nowadays is cut off from the newer development by the A23 trunk road. Used for transporting workers around the construction site, it also carries its own spare wheel alongside the driver's cab. Initially disposed of by London Transport to F.Cowley, dealers of Salford, Lancashire, it was to return north in May 1958 to W.Forshaw of Bolton for scrapping. (R.Hobbs)

Originally entering service as a Country Area 41 seat bus in March 1953 and identified by fleet number RF515, NLE515 now serves as a Green Line coach carrying fleet number RF296. It is seen here on 22nd June while in use on a private hire outing to the Ascot races. The bus had been converted for its new role, renumbered and reclassified in April 1956 and upon its first visit to Aldenham for overhaul in March 1957 re-entered service with seating for 40 passengers. Throughout its life span with London Transport and later London Country Bus Services, this combination of body number 8692 and chassis stayed faithfully married together. It is now again in the preservation movement having moved in and out over the years since disposal in September 1974. (A.R.Packer)

Overhauled in January 1957, RTL291 was reallocated to Seven Kings garage and it presents a neat picture as it stands framed by the still leafless trees at the 'Maypole', Chigwell Row while working Route 150. This route originated as a single deck operated works service between Barkingside and Hainault in 1947 and after many changes and an eighteen month disappearance in the eighties still serves this terminus, albeit at present with the blue and green buses of Harris Bus. (D.A.Ruddom collection)

In the vicinity of T.Burrows & Sons' garage at Wombwell on 12th July, BGO161 might not immediately be recognised as the chassis of ex-STL1246, especially as it now carries a Strachan lowbridge body. The bus looks smart in red livery broken by three bands of white and a Clarkson's Bitter Beer advertisement of classic lines which it was to keep for its new lease of life until demoted to a tree lopper. (A.R.Packer)

Hitchin garage on 20th August complete with its 1955 rebuilt roof which allowed double deck operation from the tiny structure situated on the corner of Park Street and Bridge Street. An RT can just be made out within the interior gloom. At the time of its closure in April 1959 with the opening of the new Stevenage garage, three GS, twelve RF and eleven RT had to be re-housed, the majority moving to the new garage although two RFs were transferred to Luton and one RT to Grays. An array of notices is evident with a neat and comprehensive timetable display on the right of the doorway, useful but odd in that no bus actually stopped at this point. (A.G.Newman)

Green Line liveried RF282 in use on bus route 458 with running plates WR50 waits for departure complete with its two men crew from Uxbridge for Slough Station. Still in its 39 seat configuration it was one of the earliest disposals of this particular version of the class and was to see further service with Premier Travel Ltd. of Cambridge. (A.Mortimer)

The history of ex-D95 commenced in June 1945 when it entered service at Merton garage, then fitted with Brush 56 seat highbridge bodywork. In 1954, after passing through the hands of a dealer, it was acquired by Southend Corporation and received a new Massey low height body seating 55 passengers, as did another twelve of the class which had been purchased. Numbered 274 it was to continue in passenger service until passing to the Basildon Salvage Company of Basildon for scrap in November 1963. It is seen in Broadway Market on Route 4A while journeying to Shoeburyness Station wearing the long-standing Southend livery of light blue and cream. (A.Mortimer)

RLH63 is seen at the South Wimbledon Underground station while in use on Route 127 and en route for St.Helier carrying running plates AL4. An RT has pulled up very closely behind at this bus stop where road space is at a premium with the intersection just out of sight to the left. The lowbridge bus had entered service at Harrow Weald in December 1952, receiving an overhaul in September 1956 from which it was returned to service at Merton. Transferred back to Harrow Weald in August 1958, it was to receive further overhauls in June 1961 and October 1965 always returning to its original garage. In July 1969 it was taken out of service and disposed of in the following month, being immediately shipped to the USA where it has had a chequered career. (A.B.Cross)

With made up route bills in a style resembling Green Line displays and GD235 running plates, RT650 is seen at Biggin Hill operating as a relief on Route 410 and about to journey south to Westerham from the air display at this former World War II Battle of Britain aerodrome. Buses were culled from far and wide for this annual event and in this case a resident of Leatherhead garage has been drafted east. (Alan Mortimer)

Gleeson, a contractor of Meadowhead, Sheffield acquired ex-Q79 in April 1956 via F.Cowley, dealers of Salford, Lancashire who had taken thirty three of the class from London Transport during August and September 1953. The bus managed just one year in use with its new owners and then, together with Q63 with a similar disposal history, languished deteriorating on the owner's premises until sold for scrap in 1960.

STL1409 first entered service in June 1936 as a 3/9STL11 operating from Merton garage. It ended its passenger career with London Transport at Hornchurch garage in March 1954 and was despatched to the dealer, W.North, in the following month. Vokes Ltd., filtration and silencing engineers of Normandy, halfway between Guildford and Aldershot, acquired the vehicle in September of the same year. They added a fine array of additional lighting and horns mounted on a metal girder fixed between the side members and gave the bus a new colour scheme. Three years later Strainwire Fencing Co. of Alton, Hampshire made further use of the vehicle but then the trail goes cold and nothing further is documented. (A.B.Cross)

Lunchtime at the Bank reveals office workers making their way to a convivial midday break. The building on the left of the picture with the massive portico is the Royal Exchange founded in the 16th century although the current building dates from 1844 when it was opened by Queen Victoria. RTL197 journeying to Shepherds Bush Green by way of Route 17 hides the lower façade of No.1 Cornhill built in 1905 for the former Liverpool & London & Globe Insurance Company whose name is still on the building. The columns of the Mansion House on the right of the picture complete a familiar but interesting architectural scene. A Ford Anglia 100E, two Austin taxis and what looks like a Scammell Scarab behind the bus add further interest. (C.Carter)

After its initial foray to Maastricht, Holland in June 1954, RT4760 settled down at Cricklewood garage for normal passenger service until called to Aldenham for its first overhaul in January 1958. It is seen here at Victoria Station on 6th April while in use on Route 16 with destination blind set for its next duty to the Crown at Cricklewood, following the path trod by motorbuses from Victoria ever since the Associated Omnibus Company extended their Victoria service from Kilburn to Cricklewood on 2nd December 1905. (A.R.Packer)

Former T613, newly repainted and converted for its new use with the British Voluntary Refuge Relief Organisation, is posed for the camera outside Westminster Abbey in January before departure on its welfare work. Today tourists throng this forecourt to enter the Abbey or purchase souvenirs from the shop and it is inconceivable that such a shot could be set up now. Nothing relating to the further use of the vehicle or the locations it visited has been found in transport history papers except that in February 1958 it was noted at Selwood's Plant Hire Depot at Chandlers Ford, Hampshire. (L.T.Museum 440/113)

The AEC Monocoach registered NLP635 was a revolutionary designed vehicle which used AEC components married to the underframe of a Park Royal body, dispensing with the traditional independently manufactured chassis and side member. Although never owned by London Transport it was on long term loan from the manufacturer for evaluation work. Arriving in July 1953 it worked on Route 447, then moved on to Green Line route 711 and in December was transferred to Dalston for Route 208 until April 1954. It returned for further trials in January 1956 which lasted until May 1957 when it was acquired by the West Monmouthshire Omnibus Board. On 29th July it is seen in Blackwood, Mons. on a service to Oakdale, still in London Transport green livery with running plate holders but with its previous operator's fleet name removed. It was sold in May 1967 for further passenger use but by March 1968 was noted in a scrapyard at Amblecote, Staffordshire. (A.R.Packer)

RT632 spent several months garaged at Addlestone during 1957 after many years at Leatherhead and prior to a move to Windsor in February 1958. Seen working Route 420 to West Byfleet, having commenced its not too taxing journey from Woking, it has plenty of room for the waiting queue of passengers should they all wish to take advantage of this nine year old vehicle. (R.H.G.Simpson)

RT4072 is seen at the Woodcote Green Post Office sometime in the early months of the year with new growth showing on the severely pruned trees lining Woodcote Road. An irresponsible motorist has parked his Ford Prefect E493A with a February 1953 registration beside the bus stop, forcing the Croydon driver of the Route 234 bus journeying to Selsdon to stop short in an otherwise deserted road. (A.Mortimer)

Performing a Railway Emergency Service duty and loaned to New Cross garage from Chelverton Road, Putney for the purpose, RTL1379 complete with crew waits for passengers while standing beside the temporary dolly stop. At present the location is unknown but the shop alongside offers a new cover and frame for your umbrella in one hour at a price starting from 27/9d (roughly £1.39). When you think about it there could only be the handle of your original brolly left!

The inspector looks as if he is writing a serious report about something. Hopefully it is not concerning the driver of T780 as he waits on the Rainham Church stand before doing another eight-minute trip down to Rainham Ferry on Route 375. This route, which originated with independent operators, survived until June 1959. Although there is still an industrial complex down by the river, public transport no longer seems to be a necessity. The bus is one of the 15T13 Mann Egerton bodied AEC Regals which were the last half cab single deck vehicles purchased by London Transport and now in its last year of operation.

New to Leatherhead in September 1948, RT631 now carries a later non-roof box body and is at Hertford Bus Station on 26th March working from the local garage. Route 395A from Hertford to Fanham Common at Ware had certain journeys which worked through from Watton Station, which in 1957 was a disused station, but there is no way of telling whether this bus has come from there. With the October Country Area changes these journeys would be left to the 390. (W.R.Legg)

RM1 with its revised frontal grille re-entered service from Cricklewood garage on 6th March, initially with advertising to the fact that the 'Routemaster' was London's bus of the future only along its length, the front panels receiving their posters later. Route 260 on weekdays and its old haunt, the 2 on Sundays, were selected for its latest venture into passenger service. This was to terminate on 31st July when this prototype RM entered Chiswick for overhaul, re-emerging in December on training duties.

In years gone by many retired buses and coaches found varied work after a little alteration to their bodies. Today it is rather rare to find time expired p.s.vs except in a scrapyard or where the travelling community and others convert them into living accommodation or caravans. What was once STL2471, an LPTB normal height double deck bus has been drastically reduced for its new use as a convenient transporter for fairground equipment. It is seen in company with another ex-p.s.v. at Putney Common on 8th August. (W.R.Legg)

RM1 runs past Cumberland Mews on its way down Edgware Road on a trip to Aldwych on Route 260 at 11.25a.m. on 22nd March. The Church Army bookshop and Headquarters are conveniently placed next to the New Inn public house and behind the bus the Green Line coach stop carries a full complement of 'E' plates. (L.T.Museum 440/154)

RTW386 waits on the time-honoured stand within Victoria Station forecourt for Route 76 buses where, in earlier books of this series, G class buses can be seen. After Dalston's allocation was withdrawn in 1940 Tottenham always provided the vehicles for this route, the wide RTW class being long associated with it. This example awaits departure on a short working to Stoke Newington, Northwold Road. The front advertisements invite you to 'try Bon, the new coffee drink'. Since we can't remember it today, it couldn't have been very 'bon'! (A.R.Packer)

The 406 and 406A routes made use of the RT class of bus for a great many years and RM2 only supplemented them for less than three months. Standing on the lay-by at Kingston Station terminus with Messrs. T.W.Lightfoot's caravan sales yard behind, RT1014 waits departure on Route 406A which had been introduced in 1956 and varied from its parent by serving Merland Rise and the Preston Hawe Estate, terminating at Tadworth Station. A large slipboard is carried on the front bulkhead giving minimum fare restrictions over parts of the route. On Routemasters provision for such notices was moved to above the window, allowing the passengers a better view of the road ahead.

Former STL679 was photographed somewhere in Belgium during the summer when in use as a caravan, complete with curtains, household paraphernalia and a door to the platform. Additional metal panels alter its appearance to a sort of a cross between the pre-war STF1 and a trolleybus but its LPTB STL5 bodywork is still recognisable. Previous London Transport ownership is also highlighted with fleet name painted out in typical fashion, running plate holders still in situ, a nearside dumb iron brass plate just hanging on and the familiar destination blind aperture. One wonders what was the final fate of this interesting vehicle. (M.R.M.New)

452W, comprising the 1930 built chassis of T176 with a 1940 manufactured 6½ ton stores body, has now reached the end of its working life and is seen within the scrapping fields of Bird's Commercial Motors. Miraculously the nearside brass dumb iron plate stamped with valuable information is still in place and although fleet name and legal owner's details have been obliterated with a crude paint job, the fleet number remains visible providing two means of immediate identification. A total of sixty of the pre-war built AEC Regal chassis used initially as the basis for T class coaches were converted for use in the service fleet, albeit 423W to 438W only on a temporary basis. These were vehicles converted to staff ambulances during World War II and the fifteen that remained were re-converted for passenger use during 1945. The missing vehicle had in the intervening period been rebodied for use as a lorry. (M.Rooum)

GS9 is seen in Hertford Bus Station still with an original style boarding notice in the quarter light by the saloon door. Route 329 operated between this terminus and Knebworth using country lanes for much of its journey and together with the 329A was the only route to pass close to the main entrance to Knebworth House. One man operated 39 seat RFs were eventually to replace the 26 seat buses, which during the course of a day's duty could be seen on a variety of interworked routes. (Alan Mortimer)

Ex-STL2355 is seen on the quayside at Ostend, Belgium on 9th June when in use as a mobile tea demonstration centre with Brooke Bond tea. Originally the bus had entered service in November 1937 operating from Holloway garage and carrying an LPTB built body classified STL14/1. Due to war losses twelve bodies were authorised by the Ministry of War Transport to be built and this STL in Chiswick Works for overhaul emerged in July 1941 fitted with the first of the new STL17 type bodies, numbered 430. Disposed of to Lancashire Motor Traders of Salford in September 1954 it was immediately purchased for its new role, being last seen in August 1961 still in the ownership of Brooke Bond. At some stage the body has lost the roof mounted route number box originally carried. (D.W.K.Jones)

The London Brick Company Ltd. of Stewartby, Bedfordshire operated both 'pre-war' and post-war RT class vehicles as staff transport for a number of years. Ex-RT32 and RT1499 with a further example of their fleet wait for the finishing time hooter before springing into life and dispersing the homeward bound workers. RT32 carried fleet number C17 while the Craven bodied RT1499 was identified as C3 but nowadays the latter is a regular rally entrant in LT red livery having joined the RT1 stable for further refurbishment in recent times. The brickworks, which were once a familiar sight around the Bedfordshire countryside, have in the main been closed down and this, together with private car ownership, has led to the demise of this once interesting operation.

On 5th April nicely turned out RT2971 from Old Kent Road garage stands at the Lewisham terminus in Rennell Street before departing on a shortened journey on Route 1 to Waterloo. The 'to and from Regents Park' slipboard will not apply to this duty but in all probability will be left in place. Route 1 was the subject of a 'localisation scheme' introduced on a number of routes on Wednesday 16th October which had the effect of withdrawing the service from this stand from Monday through to Friday excepting for some peak hour journeys. It was however still to be the southernmost terminus for Saturday and Sunday operation. (W.R.Legg)

GS Class buses first entered service at Hertford garage in November 1953 with the 329, 333, 333B and 388 routes being converted to the type. At the time Route 388 operated from the bus station at Hertford to Mardley Hill but with the withdrawal of Route 389 it was extended east from Hertford on 17th October 1956 to Sawbridgeworth to cover. GS72 is at Hertford midway on its journey across Hertfordshire. In the following year this bus, along with four others of the class, went on long term loan to Great Yarmouth Corporation. They returned in July 1959 and in the following November this example was returned to passenger service from St.Albans garage. (R.Wellings)

The Permutit Company Ltd., makers of water softeners, were the owners of ex-RT1487 from September 1956 through to June 1964. With the Permutit House offices and factory at Chiswick in the background the staff bus waits further use on 9th March. Minimal alterations have been made to the exterior though a complete repaint has been applied. First entering service in October 1949 garaged at Kingston, this Craven bodied bus saw further service at Norbiton, Enfield and Leyton before a period in storage and eventual sale to Bird's Commercial Motors the month prior to acquisition by its new owners. A van version of an early 1930s Austin 7 stands in front of the main entrance. (J.C.Gillham)

RT2119 standing within the Crawley garage yard carries blinds and running plates for the short cross town route 426A and in this instance shows the display for the short working to Three Bridges Station rather than the extension to Pound Hill which had been introduced the previous October. When this bus originally entered service from Forest Gate garage in February 1950 it was painted in Central Area livery. At the time it was one of six new buses with new chassis on to which bodies previously held in the float system were mounted. This example gained a Weymann product, numbered 1746. Upon its second visit to works for overhaul in July 1956 it was repainted into Country Area livery, in which colour scheme it remained until disposed of in April 1972. (A.Mortimer)

Ex-STL1815 is seen on 14th July taking part in the Soho Carnival Parade suitably adorned with garlands and various stickers relating to the pop and music industry. Onlookers in joyous mood admire the bus while the gem on the right, a Nash Metropolitan built by Austin and based on the A40 Devon model understructure, restricts the road width considerably. The bus had first entered service in February 1937 and was eventually disposed of the W.North, the Leeds dealer, in August 1955 to be subsequently purchased by Polyphoto (England) Ltd. based at Watford for use as a mobile showroom. It was finally scrapped by a dealer called Davis in South Mimms late in 1958. (R.Hobbs)

CRL4 was handed over to the London Transport Executive on 14th July and is seen here parked in a lay-by while running on trade plates. The writing in the lower corner of the nearside states: 'To carry 57 passengers, 25 lower deck, 32 upper deck', which was subsequently altered to 55 by the fitting of angled seating above the wheel arches in the lower saloon before entry into service in October. Note the repositioned registration number plate and lower height of the rear platform window, a feature shared with RMF1254 and the airport 9RM12 vehicles. The location of this picture has not been established but the ECW bodied Bristol single deck in the distance suggests it could be near the ECW works. (P.J.Snell)

This view taken at the Euston Station terminus of Route 77 shows lead bus RTL167 with SW1 running plates while parked closely behind is a Merton garaged RT on the same route. The RTL made an early exit from the capital's streets and it left these shores for the Ceylon Transport Board in January 1959. Older readers may remember the exploits of Commander Crabb, the frogman whose story was recounted in the film 'The Silent Enemy' advertised on the RTL as then showing at the Odeon, Leicester Square.

RT4346 stands at Well Hall Station, Eltham while the crew has disappeared for refreshment. Trees and shrubs in the background still await the warmth of spring before breaking into their summer greenery. The history of Route 132 can be traced back to 16th June 1926 when a service operated by Sidcup garage, assisted on Sunday by Tilling buses from Catford, first took to the roads between Lewisham and Bexley with a Sunday extension to Dartford. The present terminus had been first used on 9th September 1936 and the route became a circular operation through Bexleyheath in November 1939. (W.R.Legg)

St.Albans garaged RT3599 waits for the destination blind to be changed at Hemel Hempstead Bus Station before departure on a further 330 duty. The advertisements in the bus shelter include details of the Country Area 5/- Rover ticket and forthcoming excursions offered to Ascot Races, Epsom Races and London Airport. These excursions had been somewhat restricted at the start of the year due to fuel rationing. (Alan Mortimer)

RT114 in Country Area livery at Hertford clearly shows the unused rear roofbox peculiar to RT1 to RT151 and which had not been used since the early years of the Second World War. Except for the repanelled area where the original offside route number plate was carried and the addition of the two reflectors at the lower edge of the rear panel, the bus looks much as it did when it first entered service in Central Area livery in June 1940. When its period of passenger use at Hertford ended later in the year under review, its main duties were as a learner vehicle, though lengthy intervals of being unlicensed were encountered before its sale in June 1963. (W.R.Legg)

The TD class of bus could be seen in the year under review operating from Tottenham, Edgware, Kingston, Muswell Hill, Norbiton, Hornchurch, Leyton and Uxbridge garages. Here at the 'Windsor Arms' stop at Esher, TD112, garaged at Kingston, journeys to Ripley by way of route 215 in the early summer sunshine. However, judging by the attire of the people who have given this bus a miss, the weather was still on the cool side. At the left hand side of the picture a Ford 'Squire' is just overtaking the bus. The 'Squire' was one of two conversion of the small Ford van which could be purchased, closely linked to the 'Anglia' 100E model, being the more expensive with decorative bits of wood on the side and a slightly better trim. (R.Hobbs)

Since its transformation from a red Central Area bus to a green liveried Country Area one in December 1955, RT2779 has been garaged at Two Waters. Seen in use on the town service 320, it pulls away from the stop at the north end of Marlowes in Hemel Hempstead as it journeys to Warners End, Martindale Road via Two Waters and Boxmoor Station. The motor cycle and sidecar parked beside the kerb illustrates the lack of tread on tyres possible before the days of MOT inspections. (R.Wellings)

On 12th July in Middlesbrough ex-D28, now of Transport Motor Services, Bishop Auckland, waits with driver at the ready for further duty. This combination of Daimler CWA6 chassis and Duple 56 seat highbridge bodywork had first entered service in October 1944 from Merton garage. Withdrawn from service in September 1953 it was despatched to W.North & Sons the following month and immediately acquired by its new operator. The following year platform doors were fitted and in this guise it was to continue in passenger use until withdrawn and scrapped in 1958. (A.R.Packer)

TD117 was pictured when brand new in service from Leyton garage on page 69 of the 1949 book of this series. Some eight years later it is seen in Clarence Street, Kingston, while in use on Route 218 journeying to Staines via Laleham as running number K21. In the previous December it had received its second and final overhaul which accounts for its gleaming condition. It was withdrawn from service in January 1960 and exported to Ceylon in the March of that year. (A.Mortimer)

Standing on the stone setts of the Dock Street bus station in Dundee, situated close to the Firth of Tay, ex-STL2690 waits its next duty to Broughty Ferry via the Ferry Road. The date is 17th July and the bus still looks resplendent in its operator's colours of green and white with fleet number 174 applied soon after acquisition almost two years previous. All ten 18STL20 acquired by this operator were withdrawn in December 1964 and disposed of to a dealer by the name of Tiger in Salsburgh, near Airdrie, who managed to find new owners for three examples, scrapping the remainder. (A.R.Packer)

With the Clarendon Hotel at Watford behind, which has withstood the changes of time although now known as the 'Flag and Firkin', RT4171 is seen on peak hour service 344 on its way from Watford By Pass to the Tolpits Industrial Area. Prior to 12th June this route had run to Watford Met. Station but the growing area of industrial development down by the River Colne had brought about its diversion. At this stage it went as far as the Moor Lane crossing, turning at Olds Approach, but in July 1958 it would be cut back to the Holywell Estate. The bus was allocated from new in June 1951 to Watford High Street and then Garston until moving south to Crawley in December 1961. (R.Wellings)

RT1554 is seen in Upminster in October operating from Hornchurch garage on the very short service 249, Upminster Park Estate to Corbets Tey. For many years this route had the distinction of being London Transport's shortest and in fact the extension beyond Upminster Station to the new estate had only occurred on 21st August. Withdrawn in the cuts of August of the following year, 86A covering the new section of route, it was found necessary to re-invent the shortest route from the station to Corbets Tey in the following April in the form of a 248A. The lady with the shopping basket indulges in a little jay walking which was not too dangerous given the low level of traffic. (A.R.Packer)

GS42 is seen standing in the car park terminus at Rickmansworth L.T.Station with route blind still needing attention before departure on its next duty. It was not until 29th March 1972 that this particular bus became the very last of the class in passenger use in London after being resurrected from training duties a year earlier. Route 336A had the honour of being the final route to use these E.C.W. bodied 26 seat vehicles with Guy Special chassis. After eighteen months in the care of the Matthew Arnold County Secondary School at Ashford, GS42 moved into the preservation movement. (A.B.Cross)

The magnificent Corinthian portico of the Royal Exchange has dominated the road junction we know today as 'The Bank' since the early 1840s. It was built to replace an earlier building destroyed by fire and its design was the result of a competition. It was reckoned that the design submitted by C.R.Cockerell was superior but due to a muddle, the design of Sir William Tite was accepted and still stands today. In this March view Route 6 appears to be bunching as RTW269 chases a fellow vehicle on the route across the junction. Behind RTL599 follows on Route 9. (L.T.Museum 24552)

The 'Thorns Hotel' at Horley became the main halfway refreshment stop for both London Transport public and staff excursions to Brighton and other nearby coastal resorts when the A23 road was closed between Povey Cross and Lowfield Heath. The closure was brought about by the development of the new Gatwick Airport with the consequent loss of the two previously favoured watering holes. The new A23 was relaid further to the east to skirt the aerodrome perimeter. Most of the occupants of RT3240 'on tour from Romford' have deserted the bus to refresh themselves before continuing their journey on 23rd June. (R.Hobbs)

RT1399 attracts a few shoppers at Thornton Heath on Monday 18th March for a journey through south London and the West End to West Hampstead, West End Green. 159 was a route number born out of the 'Bassom system' of December 1924 and still operates to this day though only between Streatham and Baker Street Station, currently in the hands of Arriva, London South. (W.R.Legg)

The bus stop area is clearly defined on the road surface but only a temporary 'dolly' stop has been provided on the pavement. GS16 waits to take up further duties after the destination blind has been rewound. This particular vehicle could not settle down at any one particular garage during its twelve years in London Transport ownership and made three short stays at Amersham while at other times it saw service from at least eight others. It was disposed of in January 1966 and by 1977 was being use in a donor capacity, providing spares to help maintain GS42 in preserved condition. (A.Mortimer)

First entering service with LPTB in December 1945, G326 carried its Park Royal utility body number 949 throughout its entire existence. W.North & Sons, the dealer of Leeds, acquired the bus in March 1953 and together with three other members of the class, it joined the fleet of Lancaster Corporation, being licensed for service in August. G.P.Holder, trading as Charlton-on-Otmoor Services acquired the vehicle in April 1956 and it is seen on 28th July at the Gloucester Green Bus Station in Oxford, soon to depart for Bicester Ordnance Depot. It saw further use as a store shed while still owned by Holder, which extended its life from May 1958 until removed for scrap in March 1961. (J.C.Gillham)

Uxbridge garaged RT1154 stands at the station terminus ready for a peak hour run to Hounslow West Station on the relatively new route 198. This had been introduced on 6th January as part of a general rearrangement of services in and around the Uxbridge area. This bus, numerically the third Saunders bodied RT, first entered service in March 1949 and although having gone through two overhauls, it still carries a body of its original type. (A.R.Packer)

With a little over one year's further passenger use with London Transport to complete, RTL239 begins to show signs of neglect with bodywork damage on the cab and front dome. It waits, kept company by another Route 105 bus, with blinds set for a journey to Shepherds Bush, Wells Road at Brent Road, Southall, an area now totally redeveloped. (R.H.G.Simpson)

RT3442 waits for a new crew outside Northfleet garage before continuing its journey to Craylands Lane at Swanscombe while in use on Route 487 in February sunshine. Originally entering service in February 1952 at High Wycombe it was transferred to Luton in May 1953 and since re-entering service from its October 1955 overhaul has resided at Northfleet. (A.R.Packer)

The TD class used on Route 240A were a familiar sight at Edgware for many years. TD73, as EW2, waits on the garage approach road for its next call to service. In October 1962 conversion to double deck of routes at Uxbridge and the resultant surplus of RFs, finally lead to the end of the TD class on this their last stronghold. (A.Mortimer)

RF567 is seen at Welwyn Garden City Station on 19th January with a respectable queue of lady shoppers about to board the bus to Cole Green, Hertingfordbury and Hertford. Behind the bus Bridge Road crosses the main railway line and the rather bleak area in view is now all part of the Howard Centre shopping complex. The bus carries its original body, number 8744, and this would again be remounted on the chassis at its March 1958 overhaul, not being separated until April 1962 some nine years after it first entered service. (A.R.Packer)

RT4607 re-entered service at Hounslow after its first visit to Aldenham for overhaul which took place in January of the year under review. At Hounslow bus station it lays over on Route 81B to London Airport Central. This had been the first route to serve the newly built central terminal area via the road tunnel on 22nd May 1954, then only on a summer weekend and Bank Holiday basis. Full daily operation started on 4th April 1955. (Alan Mortimer)

Red liveried RT1601 picks up a good load of passengers for its journey on Route 495 through Pelham Road, Perry Street and Waterdales to the Plough at Northfleet. This bus had been transferred into the Country Area in December 1956 and served several months at Northfleet before returning to New Cross. A bus driver cycles past, no doubt heading for either the Maidstone & District or London Transport garage to commence duty. (A.R.Packer)

Forest Gate garaged RT3745 is seen in Putney, having just departed the terminus at the Common, and now has the long haul to Redbridge Station in front of it. The date is 14th February, just four months from its first visit to Aldenham. Notice the cost of a biro pen in 1957 at 5/9d, a high price to pay at that time for a developing new product. (W.R.Legg)

Obviously a welcome sight at St.Mary's Square, Hitchin, RF584 has arrived and is ready for the thirteen-minute journey on 364 as far as Preston rather than the full run to Luton. This is Tuesday 20th August and two such extra journeys were worked on that day of the week which was market day in Hitchin. The bus operates with a two-man crew and is still classified as a 2RF2/2 although this would change the following year in September when it was converted to one-man operation, reseated for 39 passengers and reclassified 2RF5/1. Contact with extra low tree branches over the years has inflicted damage to the front nearside dome and, coupled with the general dull appearance, it suggests that its March 1958 overhaul will not be before time. (A.G.Newman)

Harrow Weald garage was the final operational base for RT2438 before its disposal to the U.K Atomic Energy Authority who made use of the bus as internal transport at Aldermaston complete with a notice 'Not to be driven off site'. In less restrictive use it is seen waiting at Ruislip before commencing a short journey on Route 158 to Harrow Weald garage. (J.G.S.Smith collection)

GS60 originally entered service in December 1953 from Amersham garage and returned there after its first overhaul in April of the year under review. Seen soon after its sojourn at Aldenham Works it was back in use on familiar roads and here waits for departure time at the Chesham Moor terminus of Route 397. After its second and last overhaul it re-emerged in February 1962 to be garaged at Garston, ultimately being delicensed in February 1967. It was not until September 1969 that it was sold to G.C.Bickers of Goddenham before being acquired for preservation in March 1976. (A.Mortimer)

RT1989 has come to grief while in passenger service on Route 179 on a journey that should have taken it to Farringdon Street. Local children discuss the predicament now confronting them in Stanstead Road, Catford on a dreary March morning, no doubt adding the incident to their reasons for being late for school. With damage confined to the cab area, repairs were executed quickly and the bus returned to normal duties within a short time. (J.Wills)

Ex-STL1759 is seen parked in Edwin Street, Gravesend on 5th August with the typical drab background of the inner part of this Kent riverside town behind. The STL had originally entered service in January 1957 as a 4/9STL14 with body number 17055. Re-entering service in November 1938 from overhaul it then carried body number 17027 of the same classification and this combination was to stay matched together throughout its future existence. Disposed of to W.North in April 1953 it is seen in the ownership of Banfield's Coaches. (L.Rowe)

GS80 stands parked on the piece of land at the corner of Queen Street and Bridge Street in Hitchin used for parking double deck buses before the adaptation of the bus garage. Green Line liveried RF119 and an RT keep it company on 19th January. The route blind for the additional 383 service provided between Hitchin and the Purwell Lane Estate at Walsworth is carried together with running plates HN6. (A.R.Packer)

The Victoria Embankment looks most uninviting after a recent downpour of rain but the road vehicles provide interest for the intrepid photographer. RT2055 is employed on Route 109, born in 1951 as a replacement for tram services 16 and 18 in stage three of the conversion programme. Ex-RT1462 wears an entirely different livery to that previously carried and is now operated by the West Herts Coaches Ltd. of Garston. The very neat blinds displayed seem to owe something to London Transport style. All traces of the tramway reservation have now disappeared and the traditional London Austin taxi, Fordson Thames light delivery van and a 100E Ford Anglia bringing up the rear enjoy the dual carriageway now made possible. (F.W.Ivey)

The lengthy Route 410, operating between Reigate and Bromley necessitated the use of low height buses because of a low bridge encountered at Oxted station, midway between the termini. RLH36 is seen at Bromley on 20th October before departing to Reigate. The bus clearly displays its provincial pedigree by the deep radiator and sliding ventilators to three sets of windows on each deck. Other differences compared to the standard London Transport bus are the offside fuel tank and hinged driver's cab door. (A.R.Packer)

By the mid-fifties the training fleet contained many 2RT2 vehicles as represented here by RT101 garaged at Camberwell and seen at London Bridge Station in February. This particular body, number 409, is one of the small number which carried quarter drop windows, not perpetuated on the post-war members of the class but universally fitted to the later generation of RM family buses and coaches. (Michael Dryhurst)

Ex-RT1417 presents a sad sight after having been completely burnt out the previous month. Now it stands alongside an AEC chassis on 18th July at Lowlands Motorways' Shettleston garage yard. The RT chassis was repaired and despatched to W.Alexander & Sons bodyworks at Falkirk for a new lowbridge body to be fitted but for some reason this was not proceeded with and it was eventually cut up by Millburn Motors of Glasgow in December. Had it been so rebodied it would have been a unique and interesting vehicle. (A.R.Packer)

Standing at St.Mary's Square, Hitchin on Tuesday 20th August not one, but three GSs for the benefit of the fanatic followers of the class. Two Hertford buses, GS18 and GS72 flank Hitchin's GS80. As shown by its badly wound blind, GS 72 is working the short shuttle to Great Wymondley while GS18 is destined for Buntingford, which was the eastern extremity of the 386 route on Tuesdays. On Saturdays and Sundays the route worked right through to Bishops Stortford while on Thursdays only Buntingford to Bishops Stortford was served. The Hitchin bus is working the additional service on Route 383 to the Purwell Lane Estate at Walsworth. (A.G.Newman)

RFW7 is caught by the camera at an unknown location presumably on a private hire duty. This ECW bodied coach initially entered service in May 1951 and would be withdrawn by London Transport in October 1963. Its life as a coach was further extended with use in the tours department of the Ceylon Transport Board, later the Sri Lanka Central Transport Board, until withdrawn in July 1981. It was then cannibalised to provide spares for the dwindling fleet, which once numbered ten on this island in the Indian Ocean. (R.F.Mack)

Ex-STL2600, dating from 1939, is seen at Kilmarnock on 25th August with two further A1 Service buses in the background, the nearer of which is a former Craven RT. The STL was one of 132 fitted with the STL16 or 16/1 type body built by the LPTB and reckoned to be the most elegant. Seven of the batch STL2516 through to STL2647 escaped being converted to SRT configuration and were disposed of as complete entities. This example went to W.North, the dealer of Leeds, in August 1953. It was acquired immediately by the Ayrshire Bus Owners (A1 Service) of Ardrossan, the owning member being Steel of Stevenston, and ran until withdrawn in June 1958. Since acquisition a driver's cab door has been added, the original roof mounted blind box has been removed rather crudely and the front wheel arch has lost its distinctive curvature at the rear. (A.J.Douglas)

Barking's RTL762 lays over at the New Mill Inn, Romford stand before working back on the horseshoe shaped Route 87 to White Post Corner at Rainham. This deserted and tranquil scene is likely to have been a Sunday on which day half the 87 service turned here rather than running on to Gidea Park. This particular RTL was to enjoy another ten years in service before departing for the scrapping fields of Wombwell in Yorkshire. (A.Mortimer)

Red liveried RT1688 at Sevenoaks bus station on the Country Area service 402 makes do with a side/rear blind in the front via point box. Normally a resident of Catford garage, the northern terminal of the 402 at Bromley is at least familiar territory to this central vehicle. (Alan Mortimer)

An interesting view at Brentwood finds Green Line liveried RT3259 and another behind waiting their next turns on the 721 route to Aldgate. These AECs contrast with the contemporary vehicles of Eastern National, two ECW bodied Bristol Lodekkas, that opposite on Route 262 being an LD5G, registration 503EEV. At the beginning of the year under review the 1,000th Lodekka had been produced and soon 30 feet long examples were to appear. (A.B.Cross)

With the trolleybus wiring of the Ponders End terminus reflected in the upper deck saloon windows, newly overhauled RT2352 waits to re-enter passenger service on the forecourt of Enfield garage on 13th April although the blinds need a little re-adjustment, the side one showing more of the 102 route than the 107. The bus, however, looks ready for another three and a half years service before a repeat visit to Aldenham will be made in November 1960. (W.R.Legg)

Richardson Brothers of West Hartlepool had premises in close proximity to another ex-London Transport bus operator by the name of Bee-Line and STL2358 owned by the former is seen parked here with another of the class. To the left of the picture a Vulcan flat bed bodied lorry exhibits the diversity of the operator's business. After just four years in operation on industrial contract and school work the bus was returned to W. North, the dealers involved in its initial sale, this time for scrap. Although carrying two different bodies while in the ownership of London Transport the vehicles was always classified 4/9STL14/1. (R.Hobbs)

With the corrugated cladding of Dunton Green garage as a backdrop in this April scene, RF227 in Green Line livery manages to conceal the registration of the Country Area bus liveried example parked behind and in consequence its identity. With front route blind showing 704 to Dunton Green, side board for the 705 Sevenoaks to Windsor service, running plates DG204 and a paper in the second saloon window announcing 'To & From London Airport', its running number signifies its recent employment on a Green Line relief duty. One of the earliest RFs to be disposed of, it immediately saw use as one of the ten airside transfer coaches used by British Airways Corporation at Heathrow. Odd that for some years previous it had passed the Airport many times without venturing in. (P.Gulland)

The driver of well laden RLH54 gives a hand signal of his intentions to move away from the kerb in Imperial Drive on the last lap of the journey to Rayners Lane Station on 4th August. The driver of the pre-war Wolseley will have to decide whether to overtake or hold back and with age decidedly not on his side, a wise move might be to take the latter course. Harrow Weald had been the home of this Weymann low height bus since it first entered service in November 1952 and it was August 1958 when it finally broke the ties and was transferred, never to return to its old haunts. (A.R.Packer)

Park Lane, Knebworth looks very uninviting in this wintry scene with GS14 carrying the mud of the Hertfordshire lanes on its journey to Datchworth on Route 329A. This particular bus was given three overhauls by London Transport, being one of only a dozen to attain this distinction. It is now preserved, first joining the swelling numbers of this type in May 1976. (N.N.Forbes)

This view of excursion and special service buses at the Biggin Hill Air Display demonstrates the popularity of the event and the fact that public transport was still relied on for access to such occasions. The centre piece, RT1646, has just re-entered service at Elmers End garage after its August overhaul and the superb paint finish of the bus can be judged by the reflection of the inquisitive youth walking towards further parked RTs in both red and green liveries. (A.Mortimer)

Samuel Ledgard acquired a quantity of ex-London Transport vehicles, commencing with a sizeable number of D class buses in the fifties followed by an even greater number of post-war classes in the sixties. En-route for Leeds, ex-D234 in the livery of blue, two white bands and green roof passes a parked Ford Escort estate car while an Austin A35 of the larger rear window variety travels in the opposite direction. The Daimler CWA6 which arrived at its new owners in February 1953 was eventually withdrawn in February 1962 after a longer period in exile than was spent in London. Despite the fact they were never actually used, the removal of the full set of blind apertures seems to give the bus a more utility appearance than it had when working from Sutton. (R.F.Mack)

Younger readers may not immediately realise some of the countries that ex-Q type vehicles were exported to in the 1950s. Cyprus, Burma, Gold Coast, Jamaica, Libya, Malta, Spain and Yugoslavia are all known to have taken varying numbers and put them to good use. What was once Q20 is seen with Libyan registration plate LT. C115 and a very professional body conversion to meet right hand road use although the bus is still fitted as right hand drive. An attractive paint scheme has been applied together with side marker lights at roof level. (M.R.M.New)

RM2 operates on Route 406 to Redhill with running plates RG10. Commencing service on 20th May and although still in its first few days of passenger service, the absence of the 'This is London's Bus of the Future' notices which it had carried prior to entering service is noteworthy. Notable too is the word 'Route' painted above the offside route number blind box. The man in the front upper deck corner seat could well be a London Transport official observing the trials while the bus waits at the 'Red Cross' Hotel stop before continuing its journey. The vehicle had been officially taken into stock on 10th March 1955 and even after two year's exhaustive testing, problems arose with the transmission and brakes only days after it entered service. (R.Hobbs)

STL2019 had originally entered service with London Transport in February 1937 with a Park Royal body numbered 17440 and ended its passenger carrying days fitted with an LPTB built body, numbered 16989. After a period of disuse it was resurrected as a staff bus, a service it performed until June 1955. Time for disposal arrived in January 1956 and after passing through the usual dealer's hands surfaced with D.Bayliss of Creca, Dumfries and Galloway. Nothing further is known of its subsequent history except that it is seen here on 16th June with a seed merchants in the background carrying a rather un-Scottish name. (A.B.Cross)

Two buses wait new crews opposite Northfleet garage before continuing on their journeys. RT2263, having just re-entered service from its February overhaul is employed on Route 480 to Gravesend (Denton). The roof route number box variety behind, RT3626, is in service on Route 488 to Kings Farm Estate. The higher numbered RT would be disposed of in May 1964 while the lower lasted until May 1973. (A.R.Packer)

During its brief stay in the Country Area RM2 stands at Tadworth Station before returning to Kingston over Route 406A. Behind an RF also waits at the terminus on Route 435 from Leatherhead, a service which was to disappear in the winter programme of Country Area changes. By that time however the Routemaster had been rejected by the green bus operating division and was in passenger service at Turnham Green garage in Central Area livery. (Michael Dryhurst)

The familiar recognition clue, the route number plate set further towards the rear of the bus, shows that Saunders RT3/3 bodywork is now carried by RT1677, which entered service in March 1950 with a Park Royal RT8 body. This bus had arrived back from overhaul in September and is seen the following month at the familiar Bromley North terminal stand. (A.R.Packer)

Wearing a very appropriate fleet name this 9T9 made the long journey to New Zealand. T416 is seen at its new owner's depot at Point Chevalier, Auckland in October. Owners Jackson and Guinvere, who traded as Green Line Bus Services have altered the coach very little, save for discarding the life rail, altering the route box aperture slightly and repositioning the side lights. The P on the registration plate, P*762, indicates its passenger service usage, which lasted from 1953 through to 1959 at which time it was disposed of. The coach was acquired from L.W.Vass Ltd. of Ampthill, Bedfordshire who at the time handled considerable numbers of time expired London Transport vehicles, many of which were subsequently exported abroad. (D.P.Kirker)

At the Smith's Luxury Coaches garage situated in Reading, Berkshire on 26th January, ex-RT3 lacks platform doors which were still to be fitted. It had been acquired in May 1956 via Norths, the Leeds dealer, and was to manage a creditable seven years of passenger service on contract work conveying workers to and from the Aldermaston and Harwell atomic energy establishments, before eventually being withdrawn from use in 1963. It was then sold for scrap to another Smith, in this case a dealer by that name in Slough. Of special note for an independent operator is the substantially built garage and workshops and the huge parking and turning area, which can be gauged by the lowbridge Leyland PD1 and Bedford OB parked at the far edge of the compound. (A.R.Packer)

RLH15 stands in the garage yard at Guildford sometime in the summer, having re-entered service from overhaul in January at Addlestone garage. Some idea of the limited headroom afforded upper deck passengers can be judged when one compares the differing height above the bottom of the window level of the upper and lower saloons. Any long journey on the top deck of an RLH usually resulted in a crick in the neck. In London Transport ownership from June 1950 through to March 1965 this bus has now completed more years in exile, since after passing to Super Coaches of Upminster it was exported to the U.S.A. in 1967 where it has had a number of owners.

In Station Road at Upminster RLH22, almost empty of passengers, sets out on another short run to Cranham. Even on this short route it is managing to operate a short working from Upminster Station rather than Hall Lane, River Drive. Cranham was the most easterly destinat-ion reached by a London Transport lowbridge bus. In the far background the outline of the buildings of Upminster Station can just be made out with its combined L.T. and B.R. totem. (A.R.Packer)

Route 807 had been introduced on 17th October 1956 to provide a few journeys between Letchworth Station and Stevenage via some previously unserved roads through Letchworth Gate, Lannock Hill, Weston and Friends Green. GS2 travels on a northbound journey. It was an odd timetable consisting on Monday to Friday of a lone southbound journey at 6.47a.m. through to the Stevenage Industrial Area; an afternoon return journey to Trinity Church at Stevenage; a return afternoon peak journey from Gunnels Wood Road and on Saturday an afternoon return journey allowing two hours in Stevenage and an evening trip giving three and a half hours in the bright (?) lights of the embryonic new town. A Standard 8 drophead coupe passes, registered in March 1946 and one of a few manufactured in the immediate post-war era. (Ron Wellings)

A pre-war Morris car is parked in the background, as newly overhauled RT225 is about to continue its journey on Route 164 to Epsom Station from the parade of shops in St.Helier Avenue near the Rose Hill roundabout. The date is 5th August and while the buildings still stand to this day, parking is a different story providing a nightmare for anyone using the retail outlets and facilities at this busy junction of several major roads. (W.R.Legg)

With Well Hall Station as a background Bromley garaged RT439 waits its next run on Route 61. The date is Saturday 31st August and considering the bus was to receive an overhaul in April of the following year it does appear to be in extremely good external condition. The route, as today, worked at its fullest to Bromley North but this bus appears to be about to run into the garage. (W.R.Legg)

RT3987, with running plates TC4, waits departure at Thornton Heath for Chipstead Valley via Route 166 on 13th February. On the far right of the picture can be seen some 'pre-fab' dwellings while the immediate background is still scarred from wartime enemy action and awaits transformation. This route number had previously been used for a local service in the city, which in its final form operated between Elephant & Castle and London Bridge via Aldwych. The last day of operation of this route was 22nd September 1939 and the number lay unused throughout the war. It reappeared on 7th April 1948, being a renumbering of the weekday working of the 59. (W.R.Legg)

RT3523, with in the background a post-war Ford Prefect from the 1946/7 era and an early 1930s Morris, lays over at Romford, London Road garage between journeys on Route 370. Grays garage had been the home of the bus since re-entering service from its first overhaul in January 1956, the bus having previously been allocated to St.Albans. Yet to come was a spell at Hertford garage before an early departure from London Transport to pastures new in and around West Hartlepool with Bee-Line Roadways (Teeside) Ltd. (Alan Mortimer)

The 457C route operated journeys at appropriate times from Uxbridge Station to the main entrance of the Pinewood film studios. RT992 is seen on 22nd April at the Uxbridge terminus before departing on the short journey to its destination on Pinewood Road. Route 457D provided a similar works service through from the other direction of Slough and Windsor. This particular RT made a fairly early exit from London's country sphere of operations exchanging them for the rather more harsh conditions in Ceylon. (A.R.Packer)

One of the earlier tasks undertaken by newly overhauled RT2508 was as a Green Line relief in use on service 701 complete with running plates NF201. The date is 4th May and resting beside the exterior of Gillingham Street, Victoria garage it is kept company by Hitchin garaged RT3522 which has completed similar duties on Route 716. The front advertising carried by the lead bus provides us with a clear indication of how times have changed from the days when a £1 premium bond could be purchased with a top monthly prize of £1,000. As this book is being compiled the minimum purchase is now £100 with a monthly prize of a million pounds. (W.R.Legg)

With radiators shielded against adverse weather conditions, RT4049 and RT4038 are seen parked in the yard at Dartford garage. RT4049 nearest the camera is blinded for local route 499 which operated between Dartford, Westgate Road and Bow Arrow Lane on the Temple Hill Estate. RT4038 displays blinds for the u-shaped route 467 which operated between Sidcup and Horton Kirby via Dartford. (W.R.Legg)

The adequate country town bus and coach station provided at Dorking is sadly but a memory nowadays with the adjacent garage having been demolished and the whole site re-developed. Here, in happier days, Leatherhead's RT3632 waits departure on the long haul on Route 470 to Chelsham with two RF coaches parked in the distance in use on Green Line services 712 and 713. In this October view the double decker carries the incentive of a happy Christmas if you buy the Star newspaper and enter some sort of competition. Nothing changes! (A.R.Packer)

On 31st August, in company with an RF in use on Route 228 and another RT on the 132, Weymann bodied RT1273 exhibits the silver finish to the front axle having earlier in the month re-entered service from its second overhaul. In November 1949 when this fleet number was first sighted on the streets of London in use from Old Kent Road garage, it was identified as a 3RT3/3 carrying Saunders bodywork. The destination blind is set for Orpington Station and proves that Sidcup garage took great care of their blinds as it is one of those made in the 1950-51 period with the suffix 'ONLY' for short workings - in this case properly used. (W.R.Legg)

The immediate building beside RT4607 display majestic qualities associated with the town of Windsor, while the bus expresses its classic lines, long associated with London Transport. Working the week-end extension of Route 81 on 15th October, the bus waits to return to Hounslow garage. As usual the Guinness advertisement shows originality related to its site on the side of a bus. (A.R.Packer)

Overhanging branches in Park Lane East, South Park at Reigate receive attention from the pruners on the top deck of 969J which will no doubt benefit the RTs then operating Route 430. One operative can be distinguished with loppers held high about to displace an offending branch into the cavernous upper deck of the body of the 'Tree Pruning Equipment'. A red flag placed between the radiator and rolled up blind gives notice of danger immediately around the vehicle which was once front entrance STL1503 until its conversion in December 1952. (R.Hobbs)

Saunders bodied RT4241 is seen at Ealing Broadway on 16th June while in use on a Route 65 journey to Chessington Zoo. The T.Walton (London) Ltd. retail shops were renowned for the choice and quality of their fresh produce, especially fruit, and operated a free home delivery service as demonstrated by their delivery bicycle propped against the kerbside. Careful inspection reveals that no security devices are in evidence on the bicycle to stop a stranger removing it in those more civilised days. (A.R.Packer)

Previously Merton and Loughton garages had used this bus in passenger service although since re-entry into service from overhaul in February, RT3824 has resided at North Street, Romford. It is seen on the still new looking Harold Hill Estate operating on Route 247A, a route which had come into existence on 6th December 1950 to provide a service into the heart of the developing estate and was given the A suffix to distinguish it from the Collier Row - Brentwood operation. Both routes were operated in 1950 by the G class buses then garaged at Hornchurch. (A.Mortimer)

RT373 is seen at Upminster on 26th October starting out on its long journey through east London to Limehouse, Eastern Hotel. Originally it had been one of the batch to enter service at Cricklewood garage in March 1948, displacing STs and STLs from various routes, notably 13 and 240. After its second overhaul in August 1955 it re-entered service at Upton Park where it was to reside until a month before its next visit to Aldenham for further attention. (A.R.Packer)

RF364 stands within the Hounslow bus station awaiting its next journey on Route 237 to Chertsey Station on the running schedule AV6. As with all the Central Area variety of the RF class, no saloon door is fitted at this stage and a conductor will be available to take your fares and have his feet trampled on. RF359 to 388 were registered MXX1 - MXX30. This was before the days when such registrations attracted a premium. (A.Mortimer)

These two 'roofbox' vehicles stand at Clapham Common before departing north on Route 35 to Highams Park or right through to Chingford Hatch. RT2398 above carries an early RT3 type body built by Park Royal in 1947. Distinctive are the deeper valence to the canopy and the pillar route number plate on the corner of the bulkhead. Below, RTL36 now carries an RT10 body which was originally coded RT3 but which has been modified enabling it to be placed on a Leyland chassis. The later RT3 bodies such as this had a shallower valence which allowed the route number plate to be moved to a position below the canopy, although in this case the 35 plate is not carried, if indeed Camberwell possessed any, since most of their RTLs had no need for them. The RTL left LT ownership in June 1958 while the RT soldiered on until January 1964. (Both W.R.Legg)

RT465 was delivered with a Weymann built RT3 body but since its overhaul in August 1955 it has carried this Park Royal manufactured RT8 example and has been garaged at Turnham Green. Seen on 3rd January while in use on Route 91 it waits to depart for Hounslow West Station while in the company of an RTL on Route 28. Upon overhaul in April 1959 the chassis was re-united with an RT3 body resulting in its early disposal. (W.R.Legg)

On 20th October RT273 is seen at Sidcup working Route 229 to Orpington Station. This route had commenced operation on 10th January 1951 using two SRT class buses to operate a local service in Sidcup from the garage at Foots Cray to Wren Road. In October that year the SRTs gave way to STLs and RTLs and the route was extended to Orpington, providing a service to the St.Pauls Cray Estate en-route. (A.R.Packer)

RT1734 is seen in George Street, Croydon not far into its journey from South Croydon to Oxford Circus. Route 12 at this period in its history was operated with buses from Elmers End garage, where currently this RT is housed, Rye Lane, Croydon and Shepherds Bush. Such a lengthy and sectionalised route understandably involved a variety of garages. (A.Mortimer)

RF442 entered passenger service in February 1953 operating from Dalston garage and was to see service at a variety of garages, ending at Kingston at the time of its withdrawal in April 1977. On 20th October it is seen at Sidcup while in use on Route 228 from Eltham to Chislehurst, 'Gordon Arms'. Conversion to o-m-o operation would eventually involve addition of doors and a reduction of seating but at the present time it operates in original condition apart from the newly fitted trafficators. This addition had first appeared in 1956 and was based on those fitted to the prototype RM vehicles. (A.R.Packer)

Route 376A was a works service operating between Whipsnade or Studham, Kensworth and the AC Delco Works at Dunstable. RT1044 waits time at the 'Farmer's Boy', Kensworth before heading for Dunstable. The 356 and 376 group of routes were swallowed up by extensions of the 364 group in 1959. (R.Wellings)

Reigate's RT2509 pauses at Crawley old town while in use on Route 405, which in 1957 operated between West Croydon and Horsham, the most southerly town reached by London Transport at the time. RT3670 parked by its side will head in the opposite direction to West Croydon and is one of Crawley garage's contribution to the jointly worked route. (A.R.Packer)

On 27th October newly overhauled RTL1512 is viewed at the Crystal Palace terminus while in use on Route 3. In line with the policy of the time, the bus returned to Chalk Farm garage, which had been its home since initial entry into service in May 1954 and from where it was to operate until its next overhaul, which took place in November 1961. A 'to and from the Zoo' slipboard is carried although in practice this meant something in the region of a brisk five minute walk from the route's nearest point. Note the still silver chassis and mechanical units of the underframe which confirm its recent re-entry into service. (W.R.Legg)

On its journey to Bromley garage, RT1109 is seen at Sidcup on 20th October while in use on Route 51. Owned by London Transport between February 1949 through to June 1970 the bus was afforded four overhauls and Weymann and Saunders bodywork was carried at different times, the example shown being Weymann body number 8624 of much younger age than the chassis. (A.R.Packer)

TD69 waits in the forecourt at Edgware station before another short working trip on Route 240A to Mill Hill Broadway. The scene is completely deserted save for the one occupant of the Standard 8 saloon and suggests a Sunday working. In the following year this bus began a period of use on learner duties in an era when the 2RT2 was the normal type on which one could expect to receive tuition. Behind the bus the fencing shields the site of the former eastern side of the station colonnade which was demolished to make way for the new station serving the Northern Line extension to Bushey Heath. This of course was thwarted by the war and oddly this side has now been rebuilt and the western side removed to provide access to the new bus station. (J.Wills)

With Broad Street Station in the background and activity in evidence with both inspector and driver interested in moving RTW134, one must assume departure time has arrived. This terminus in Liverpool Street was always cluttered with buses, some often lacking relief drivers from Dalston garage, and duty inspectors spent much of their time directing passengers to the next likely bus to depart and then performing shunting operations. Route 11 used the RTW class of bus for many years and they were only ousted in favour of secondhand Routemasters in February 1966. (Photomatic)

In the 1946 book of this series, page 48 shows STL2662 with Route 362B blinds standing at the identical spot beside High Wycombe garage in which, eleven years later, RT3209 with Route 363 blinds finds itself. The front and side route blinds have had the old terminal qualification of 'The Dolphin' painted out since the route had been extended to Tyzack Road in the previous year. (Alan Mortimer)

The date is 9th September and GS81 is seen at the Carfax, Horsham terminus before departing for Crawley with running number CY24. route 852, which ran via Lambs Green, was eventually withdrawn on 3rd October 1965, not being replaced although the direct service 405 between the two towns was still maintained. The GS had been withdrawn from service some three years earlier, although it was not sold until October 1964. It is documented as being acquired by the Tideway School, Newhaven in 1971 but its subsequent fate is not known at present. (J.C.Gillham)

Even after the Second World War Route 238 remained as a one-man operated service with Cubs. However, after graduating through larger single deckers in 1949, RTs were introduced in May 1954 although the three TDs then operating the service were replaced by a single RT. Final withdrawal came on 20th August 1958 as part of the first stage of the Central bus cuts introduced after the disastrous strike of that year. In the previous year RT957, which had re-entered service at Hornchurch after its December 1956 overhaul, waits for departure time from the 'Pentowan' at Noak Hill. Hopefully the driver will remember to change the blind to Emerson Park. (A.Mortimer)

On 22nd May T749 stands beside the passenger shelter provided for those wishing to travel from Uxbridge Station on Route 222. The slipboard beneath the canopy advises that a minimum fare of 6d exists on Route 222 between Hounslow Central Station and Harlington Corner, 'Coach & Horses'. The batch of fifty AEC chassis fitted with Weymann bodywork which were the first new single deck vehicles to enter service with London Transport after World War II, were conveniently given fleet numbers T719 through to T768 although they bore little resemblance to their pre-war predecessors. (A.R.Packer)

The bus and coach parking area at Whipsnade Zoo is much more likely to be devoid of any vehicles nowadays such is the situation with the all-conquering motor car. Photographs exist showing long lines of London Transport vehicles, such as on page 107 at this Bedfordshire attraction often with very few cars to keep them company. With this particular print however the change from one mode of transport to another is clearly illustrated with the car park seen behind the buses. Most prominent of the cars is a Ford 10 on this Easter Sunday, 21st April. Green Line liveried RT3228 of London Road, Romford garage has arrived on Route 726 again re-introduced by the Country Area as part of the summer programme. The Central Area is represented by Holloway garaged R195 on excursion duties. (R.E.Stevens)

In 1957 buses required to operate Route 29 were provided by West Green and Potters Bar on a daily buses with Palmers Green garage being involved on Sundays. Leyland engined vehicles were provided in the form of RTLs by WG while AD and PB supplied RTs. RT4395 from Potters Bar attracts increasing numbers of passengers for a through Sunday journey on 13th January which will eventually reach Clare Hall Hospital at South Mimms although it is doubtful if any of these passengers will remain on board that long. Returned to service the previous month after overhaul at Aldenham the bus carries Park Royal body 8451 of the same RT8/2 type as that with which it initially entered service in October 1953. (W.R.Legg)

To meet the needs of the overhaul cycle of red RF buses a number of surplus Country Area cousins were transferred to Sidcup to maintain services commencing in September 1956. This was not the first time that green buses had been used on Route 241, several green liveried 5Q5s being used on the route in the late 1940s. Green liveried RF576 exchanges passengers at Sidcup before continuing its journey to Sidcup garage. The bus left Sidcup for overhaul in the following January. Interestingly the passenger saloon doors fitted to the temporary loans were left in the open position to satisfy police regulations in the Metropolitan area. (A.R.Packer)

With the low angle of the sun making photography difficult, RT3655 waits for a refreshed crew outside Leatherhead garage on 2nd March. The departing crew head into the garage having brought the bus from Bookham Station, its southern terminus. (W.R.Legg)

T757 is seen on 16th June as it disgorges passengers at the conveniently placed bus stop for both shoppers and those about to make use of the District Line station at Ealing Broadway. A double ended, so called 'lazy', blind is displayed emphasising the shortness of Route 211 which in 1957 only operated to the 'Red Lion' at Greenford via Gordon Road, Drayton Green Road, Greenford Avenue and Ruislip Road. (A.R.Packer)

Now fitted with a Saunders RT3/3 body replacing its original Park Royal RT8/2 example, RT4809 re-entered service from its September overhaul at Loughton previously having been allocated to Alperton garage since new in March 1954. Entering Piccadilly Circus in an orderly fashion, a ubiquitous Volkswagen Beetle overtakes the bus while following can be seen a baby Fiat 500 and a Hillman Minx Series II.

A variety of vehicles is shown in this picture of the Beeline Roadways Ltd. premises at West Hartlepool, the two with which this book is concerned being the AEC chassised examples. Ex-STL749, taking centre stage, had been acquired via W.North, the Leeds dealer, in July 1956 and was to pass to A1 Roadways of Rithwell, Leeds less than two years later solely for its engine. the remains passed to Rogers, a dealer of Churwell, for scrap in May 1958. Single deck FXT386 parked against the wall in the background started life as STL2663, an LPTB 56 seat double deck bus in March 1942. The chassis was new although the body fitted, numbered 13694, dated from December 1933 initially being mounted on the chassis of STL254. Disposed of to W.North in January 1956, the ageing body was removed and the chassis acquired by Beeline who fitted the secondhand Strachan bodywork using the resulting hybrid on contract work until it passed to Richards Westgarth Ltd of West Hartlepool for use as a mobile test laboratory. (R.F.Mack)

Garston's RT647, in its tenth year of service, waits for departure from Uxbridge Bus Station to make the lengthy journey to Hemel Hempstead on Route 347. In 1964 the bus, fitted with a roof box body acquired on its May 1960 overhaul, would be exported to South Africa. (Alan Mortimer)

The date is Easter Sunday 21st April and the location Whipsnade Zoo on one of those occasions which attracted the attention of the London bus enthusiast when so many buses were used to bring the animal lovers to this beautiful park set in the Chilterns. From left to right the vehicles lined up in military style are RTs 3228, 195, 572, 2554, 245, 3253, 3236, 3250, 3244, 3247 and 3234. The three roof box examples and the one between them are red liveried from a variety of Central Area garages while all the others are Green Line residents of Romford, London Road and in service on Route 726. RT245 was the first to be disposed of by London Transport, this taking place in February 1958 to be followed by RT572 in November 1963 while the others were to continue in passenger service for a much longer period. (R.E.Stevens)

The three blinds of RT1044 all agree that the bus is scheduled to leave Hertford Bus Station on 26th March for Bishops Stortford via the route of 350A but the canopy blind shows 350, which went via Wareside rather than St.Margarets and Hunsdon. The two routes had been extended in Bishops Stortford to the Havers Lane Estate in October 1955 and in order to fit the wordy destination in, the blind compilers have taken the unusual step of using a three line qualifying point. (W.R.Legg)

Deserted RT4696 is seen resting between trips on its SP7 schedule on Route 51 at Sidcup on 20th October. Initially entering service at North Street, Romford garage in January 1954 it never ventured elsewhere until sent to Sidcup after its first overhaul which had taken place earlier in the year under review. (A.R.Packer)

This rear end view of Mann Egerton bodied T779 illustrates the unusual design whereby the rear saloon window was lined up with the top of the rear seats. Although the front and side geometry of the batch of thirty bodies were of a well balanced design of straight lines and right angles, the style of a rounded framed window and rising paint line gave the buses an oddly old fashioned look when seen from this end. This green liveried bus was only in passenger use at Norbiton for just over six months until delicensed in March of the following year. (A.B.Cross)

TD18 was always allocated to Muswell Hill until its very last year of London Transport operation, when it was transferred to Kingston. Alongside British Railways rolling stock on 22nd May it waits departure from Kingston Station by way of Route 216 through Sunbury. The destination 'STAINES via SUNBURY' distinguished the route from the longer 218 service which carried 'STAINES via LALEHAM' although oddly both routes just showed 'KINGSTON' in the reverse direction. This bus eventually saw further service in Ceylon leaving British shores in August of the following year. (A.R.Packer)

Some lovely old ornamental iron railings are still in place in front of the People's Hall of the Evangelical Free Church at Plumstead Common in this picture taken on 3rd August. RT1161 from Catford garage cools off before setting out again on its 98 minute journey across south London to Selsdon, Farley Road. (W.R.Legg)

RF255 is seen in Sidcup on 20th October operating with running plates DT80 although officially garaged at Staines since October 1956, which was to last until its visit to Aldenham in February 1960 for overhaul. This version of Route 725 had been introduced on 1st July 1953 as the capital's first orbital Green Line service and proved extremely popular. Recent proposals to withdrawn its present day descendant Route 726 met with vehement protests and the service continues in the hands of Capital Logistics. (A.R.Packer)

Lowland Motorways of Shettleston, Glasgow purchased RTs 1417, 1418, 1457, 1461, 1484, 1501 and 1509 during 1956 and 1957. Ex-RT1418 is seen on service to the outer suburb of Barlanark and rides the cobbles and tram rails within the city centre of a system replaced by the motorbus on 4th September 1962. The business of Lowland was formally acquired by Scottish Omnibuses Ltd. on 13th January 1958 together with 36 vehicles, which included six of those mentioned above. Unfortunately RT1417 (see page 73) had been burnt out in June of the year under review and its remains despatched to Milburn Motors of Glasgow for scrap. (F.W.Ivey)

At Well Hall Station on 5th April, having recently returned to service from overhaul, RT2301 is seen in use on Route 21A waiting departure for the 'Bull' at Farningham. The driver with the help of the conductor will need to continue the use of hand signals but the driver of RF500 alongside on Route 228 has the advantage of newly fitted trafficators on his bus. This RF was one of thirty eight of the class which, together with eighty seven RTs, were fitted with this modification. The so-called 'ears' first began to appear in 1955. The decision to fully equip the fleet with them was taken in 1957 but it was not until 1959 that they began to appear universally throughout the fleet. . (W.R.Legg)

RT1153 had entered service in February 1949 from Muswell Hill garage, being the second Saunders bodied RT delivered. Two overhauls later it still carries bodywork from the Beaumaris works on the Isle of Anglesey. During their life span with London Transport none of the 300 bodies built by this manufacturer were ever mounted on an RTL chassis and therefore there was no need for the front cab structure to be modified with an upward turn in the dumb iron area. Having said that, a few examples are known to have received standard Park Royal or Weymann cab fronts with this difference. This picture is taken at the Dulwich end of the long standing 78 route to Shoreditch via Tower Bridge. (W.R.Legg)

Alperton garaged RT675 stands beside the industrial buildings at the Hayes terminus before departure on a short working of Route 83 to West Hendon. The RT3 body, number 1933, had been mounted initially on the chassis of RT654 and re-entered service on this chassis at the time of its January 1956 overhaul. (J.Gascoine collection)

GS6, with to its right GS8 are seen on 20th February parked in the Chelsham garage yard, having both received their first overhauls the previous year. Neither of these two vehicles have survived into the preservation movement. Route 464, which interworked with the 465 and 485 had been converted to GS operation in October and November 1953 with the initial deliveries of the class and it was not until 18th June 1962 that replacement came in the shape of one man operated RFs. Both vehicles were disposed of in 1963 for further use and although the lower numbered was advertised for sale in November 1974, nothing further has come to light. GS8 was sold for scrap in 1975. (W.R.Legg)

On 11th October 1953 the first use of route number 44A for a Sunday only service between Charing Cross and Mitcham was inaugurated. Standing at the 'Cricketers', Mitcham the driver of Wandsworth garaged RTL1115 is engaged in changing the destination blind for a return journey to central London. The roof damage will probably stay until the bus visits Aldenham in October of the following year for its second and final overhaul after which it would return to service looking almost brand new with body number 5710. Cigarette advertising for 'Woodbines' is carried on the front panels in the days when government health warnings were unheard of. (N.Rayfield)

RTL220 was one of the earliest of the class to be disposed of after just a little over nine years operation within the capital. Having entered service at Shepherds Bush in May 1949 it received an overhaul in March 1953, re-entering service at Walworth. A further visit to the main works for its second and final overhaul took place in May 1956 after which it was allocated to Tottenham for its final sojourn before being delicensed in August 1958 and shipped to Ceylon in December. Route 67 was also withdrawn in the same August but before this double event the bus is seen in happier times at the Waterloo bus park on 16th March. (A.R.Packer)

This use of route number 232 had only been introduced to the roads of the capital on 12th October 1955, the number having lain dormant since 27th November 1940. It operated between Hounslow garage and Greenford 'Civil Engineer' replacing parts of the 111 and 120A and used RTs garaged at Southall. A nasty dent has befallen the nearside wheel arch of RT2118 but otherwise the bus looks tidy enough. The chassis of this bus when new was fitted with a Weymann body, number 1694, which at the time was in the works float system and it entered service from Forest Gate garage in February 1950. After two overhauls it now carries Park Royal body number 2213.

RT3692 stands in the morning sunlight at the Putney Bridge Station terminus of Route 85 on 22nd May. The bus is now fitted with one of the last 150 RT3 type bodies which were built with higher canopy, trafficator holders, bulkhead route number plate and upswept cab front in the dumb iron area. New in April 1953, it has always carried Central Area livery but at its August 1963 overhaul it would be outshopped in Country Area colours, which it then kept for the rest of its passenger use with London Transport. (A.R.Packer)

Q214 was purchased direct from London Transport by Tiltman Langley Laboratories Ltd., an aeronautical engineering company who used the vehicle within the grounds of Redhill Aerodrome. It is seen on 11th August with some internal modifications having been made and a packing case inconveniently placed hiding its registration. After use as a test equipment vehicle it was sold for scrap to C.Harber of Masons Bridge Road, Earlswood, Redhill in 1959. (R.Hobbs)

T747 waits at Uxbridge on 22nd May for its next trip on Route 224 to Laleham, a journey which would involve using buses of more than one operator to achieve nowadays. The slip in the first saloon window announcing 'To and From London Airport' is a bit of a generalisation considering the route skirted the perimeter only in the Longford area and didn't venture into the rapidly developing centre of activity. (A.R.Packer)

An interesting scene on the forecourt of Cricklewood garage is provided by this picture of RTW81, RT3014 and RM1. The latter had re-entered service on 1st March after nearly seven months spent within Chiswick Works while modifications and improvements had been carried out, the grille being the only visible sign of these changes. While the RT and the RM are Cricklewood based buses the RTW is a resident of Clay Hall. Note the clocking in cards adjacent to the time clock on the extreme right of the picture. (K.Lane)

The emergency replacement Green Line coach RF22 was initially transferred to Gillingham Street, Victoria during December 1956 to be available as a replacement for any vehicle which was in difficulties within Central London. It is seen here a year later in December while in use for a defective 708 coach and is viewed in King Street, East Grinstead. The Green Line inspector, hands in pockets, contrasts sharply with the smartly uniformed soldier. This coach remained at GM until taken out of passenger service for a short while on learner duties and was then despatched to Aspec Travel, a dealer of Ilford, in May 1963. (A.R.Packer)

Route 49 first appeared on the roads of London in August 1912 using De Dion type buses between Camden Town and Clapham Junction. By 1957 the famous RT type worked the service which over the intervening years has basically kept to the roads initially used between South Kensington and Clapham Junction. Saunders bodywork is now carried by RT1612 seen waiting at the Crystal Palace terminus first reached on this route by a 49A variant in February 1914. The bus had re-entered service from its August overhaul to be garaged at Streatham. The use of the 'dolly' type bus stop and lack of a route number plate beneath the canopy are notable in this picture taken on 6th October. (W.R.Legg)

Prototype CRL4 entered public service on Route 721 on 9th October having been officially handed over to the Executive by Eastern Coach Works on 14th June. Driver training, a visit to Chiswick for modification and further driver training with the Leyland engined coach occupied the intervening period. With several thousand miles of use completed the coach was transferred to High Wycombe before the year end again for familiarisation before its period garaged at Reigate commenced in early January of the following year. In the above view the coach departs Aldgate trolleybus and coach station while the lower print depicts it en-route for Brentwood. (R.H.G.Simpson (top) and A.Mortimer (bottom))

RT3683 requisitioned for the day from St.Albans finds itself in unfamiliar surroundings as it works the race day special Route 406F between Epsom Station and the Downs with running plate 223. In this picture there are not many racegoers in evidence but the substantially built shelter contains both Central and Green Line maps in a very tidy display untouched by the, as yet uncommon, graffiti vandals.

RF23 is viewed with running number ST224 on 14th September while waiting at Ascot for further use at the end of the day's horse racing as an extra coach into London on Green Line Route 701. The angle of the front wheels suggests the driver has been careful to avoid contact with the temporary structure that is in place presumably in connection with the races. RF16 through to RF25 had received Green Line livery, side route board brackets and luggage racks during 1956 and all ten were to be withdrawn from service in 1962 to be disposed of in the following year. (A.R.Packer)

RT4184 is seen on the Ingrave Road stand at Brentwood with Eastern National 1456, a 1955 built ECW bodied Bristol LD5G with full length radiator grilled on local service 262. The blind on the RT is set for the additional service on Route 339 from Coxtie Green and the rather complicated timetable for this service did allow for an hour's lay over at this point on some occasions, presumably for meal break purposes on this section which was remote from the home Epping garage. (Photobus)

With a 1936 built D2 class trolleybus, number 433 in the distance, RT3158 waits at West Croydon Station. It will shortly depart on its rather roundabout Route 411 trip to Reigate, arriving there just under an hour and a half later. By that time the trolleybus should just about be heading into Shepherds Bush on its return journey on Route 630 from Harlesden, College Park in west London. (A.R.Packer)

Remembering the unorthodox positioning of the engine when built in 1939, the number of ex-TF class vehicles which found further use is rather surprising. On 18th August what was once 34 seat, front entrance coach TF24 is now fitted with an enclosed flat platform body to which has been added a liquid storage tank. Only the cab area of the bodywork together with the chassis now remain but its unmistakable LPTB pedigree cannot be concealed. Initially disposed of to W.North of Leeds in July 1953 it was used in its new capacity by Allweather Surfaces Ltd.

Summer Sunday route 62A followed the course of its unsuffixed counterpart as far as Hainault Forest where the two services divided, the A to terminate at Chigwell Row, Maypole Inn. Sometime during May Barking garaged RTL513 with BK2 running number waits deserted in glorious sunshine at Barking for some sort of human contact before a journey to this recreation area on the north eastern outskirts of the capital. Unfortunately it still displays the weekday 62 blind, erroneously suggesting that Barkingside was served. (A.R.Packer)

The stark background to Wakefield Street bus station at Richmond has remained unchanged for many years. The LT class buses seen on page 79 of the 1947 book of this series have given way to RTLs but their north London destination of Stoke Newington is still the same. RTL367 with RTL414 a safe distance behind, wait departure. (Kevin Lane)

A nostalgic reminder of the scene which for many years greeted any London Transport vehicle photographer who ventured on to the forecourt of Victoria Station. On 2nd June RTs fill this picture and can be seen in use on Routes 10, 29, 38, 16 and 52 with the centre bus, RT1215, about to depart for Chingford, Royal Forest Hotel. It is one of the large number of the class allocated to Leyton garage who also at the time had a small number of TD single deck buses for their share of the 236 route. London Co-op advertising covers the available front space on the subject RT in the days when your Co-op 'divi' number was as important as your Visa pin number is today. (A.R.Packer)

T796 was one of a small number of green liveried 15T13s temporarily drafted into the Central Area during the year under review. During August it entered Aldenham for a further overhaul re-entering service in the Country Area at Grays garage where it continued in passenger use until June 1959 after which it was delicensed to await disposal. Here it emerges from Thorkhill road at Thames Ditton en-route for Hampton Court on Route 201 during its spell of operation from Norbiton garage in the earlier part of the year. (F.W.Ivey)

Standing in Stevenage old town on 19th January, two RTs work 'New Town Service' Routes 392 and 392A, both about to head up Julians Road to Stevenage Station, which was where it was located in 1957. Looking at contemporary timetables it is difficult to see why the two buses should have met like this but timetables were not always strictly adhered to even in those days. Both buses are in red livery, the nearer the camera being RT657 while furthest away is RT2494. They were to work in the Country Area for almost the full year and after their return to Central Area work both received overhauls within three months. The lower numbered RT will be remembered for it's out of sequence registration, its previous intended identity and original body providing the basis for RTL501. (A.R.Packer)

By a remarkable coincidence RT1591, carrying red livery, was also on a one year loan to the Country Area and was caught by the camera coming on to route from the temporary garage in Fishers Green Road at Stevenage. This bus bears the consecutive registration, KLB713, to that carried by RT657, showing at which point in production the Park Royal factory filled the gap caused by the appropriation of the original RT657. Note too the blinds showing 'NEW TOWN SERVICE', the term 'NEW' being dropped at a later stage. Also of note are the wirebound telephone communications both behind the bus and following the line of the railway to Scotland at the right. (A.R.Packer)

RT1083 passes the Old Town Hall at Reigate, seemingly on its way back to Reigate garage on a section of road where the traffic flow is now only in the opposite direction. There appear to be a couple of passengers on board although the rather strange blind display reading '406 via Main Road LONDON' can't have helped them decide this was the bus they wanted. It could in fact be a 406 extra returning from race crowd duties at Epsom. The Austin pick-up beyond the bus was based on the A40 Devon model and continued in production long after the saloon had ceased manufacture, while nearer the camera is a Morris Minor 1000 Traveller. (R.Hobbs)

RT3909 is captured in this April view at the Crystal Palace Parade terminus with RTL889 parked further from the camera. The RT, garaged at New Cross, waits departure for Woolwich, General Gordon Place on Route 186 initially introduced in July 1952. On 1st July this route would be extended on from Crystal Palace to Victoria via Tulse Hill replacing 195 in the process and providing a very convoluted way of getting from Woolwich to Victoria if you had time on your hands. The skeleton roof of the abandoned Crystal Palace High Level Station can be seen in the background behind the low brick wall. (P.Gulland)

T767 and RT2165 await further use on the parking area at Uxbridge bus station on Routes 224B and 198 respectively. Both routes had been introduced in a revision of services in the Uxbridge area on 23rd January of the year under review. 224B was the first service into the then new Stockley Estate and the 198 provided a link to Uxbridge from the Oak Farm Estate at Hillingdon. The single decker seen here was despatched to Ceylon in January 1959 for further use, while the double decker departed to be scrapped at Wombwell Diesels in March 1971. (F.W.Ivey)

This glorious procession at Apsley shows RTs in convoy on the main A41 road to take up position on the special works services for the employees soon to stream out of the paper mills complex. RT3528 leads the group with route blinds set for the short journey from the mills to Hemel Hempstead, Bathurst Road on a 316A service that had been introduced on 12th June of the year under review. The following roof box RT cannot be identified but RT4529 at the rear carries route blinds ready for its use on Route 377A which ran to Cupid Green and Markyate. St.Mary's Church and the houses remain to this day but are now reached by their own cul-de-sac, the main road being realigned out of the picture to the right. Between the second and further bus a sizeable roundabout now exists with an access road leading off to the Apsley Mills Retail Park. (R.Wellings)

RTL1032 on the left and RTW432 take on passengers at Turnpike Lane on 9th March. At this time the 231 still continued to Alexandra Park ('Victoria') and had been renumbered from 144B nearly three years previous to this photograph. 144B had been born out of the north London tram conversions in 1938 and the tram loading bays with their neat subway connections to the Underground station still provided a useful facility. Route 41 has a history stretching back much further in time, having started with B type single deckers between Muswell Hill and Crouch End via Archway in 1915. (J.H.Price)

This nearside view of ex-T656, now used as a mobile showroom by the Tri-ang toy makers, allows a glimpse through the conveniently open saloon door of the T10/1 body with waist height partition and narrow doorway. Initially a Green Line coach first entering service in October 1938, it was then converted into an ambulance in the early days of September 1939. The vehicle then passed on to the American Red Cross for conversion to a 'Clubmobile' carrying identification X201116 and named 'New Hampshire'. Returning to the LPTB in November 1945 it was to resume its pre-war duties in May 1946 and remained in use as a bus or coach within the Country Area until withdrawn from service in late 1953. (A.Mortimer)

The 386 route, together with its associated 329A and 386A, first received the GS class buses from 21st April 1954 replacing crew operated RF and 10T10 vehicles in the process. Hertford's GS10 takes on board passengers before leaving Bishops Stortford on the long through Saturday/Sunday operation to Hitchin. The driver has chosen an incorrect blind display which was more appropriate to the Tuesday operation from Buntingford to Hitchin. A small number of this class of vehicle were purchased direct from L.T. and L.C.B.S. by preservationists and this particular example was one of those in October 1973. (Photomatic)

Sometime in February RT3628 and another are about to be passed by a Maidstone & District bus while they pick up passengers in Gravesend, the most easterly town sited south of the Thames served by London Transport. Some years later the lead bus would emerge from overhaul in Central Area colours ending its long association with the Country Department. Self service in grocery shops was in its infancy in 1957 and warranted special advertising, as seen in the window display of the Price Reduction Stores. (A.R.Packer)

In this view of CRL4 looking forward in the lower deck, the arrangement of the bucket seating provided can be partly seen in the lower corners. These seats replaced the traditional longitudinal benches shortly after the coach was delivered. A number of passengers sit comfortably on the deeper cushioned, higher backed seats while above the luggage racks extend over nearly all the forward facing seating. The notice on the front bulkhead is headed 'This Double Deck Coach' but whether the interior embodies all the attributes normally associated with such a vehicle is debatable. (A.B.Cross)

RT4720 is seen at Victoria Station apart to depart for Loughton Station on Route 38A on the schedule for L8. The date is 14th January and the bus still carries its original Weymann body number 8961 with which it first entered service in March 1954 from Hornchurch garage. Before the end of the year under review a visit to Aldenham for overhaul meant the separation of the body from the chassis for ever. In the background can be seen the ornamental canopy to the front of the station with wording which reminds one of the past continental importance of this London terminal long before the days of Waterloo International and the Chunnel. (A.R.Packer)

Elsewhere in this book you will find GS72 working a short journey on Route 386 from Hitchin the Great Wymondley on 20th August. That was how the bus filled in time between journeys on the Tuesday and Saturday Route 329A from and to Datchworth. It would also operate on Route 329 to and from its home garage at Hertford. Here it waits to return to Datchworth after performing its 386 shuttle duty still with the windscreen wiper tucked away out of the driver's line of vision. (A.G.Newman)

Victoria garaged RT939 is ready to leave Crystal Palace on a journey on Route 137 to 'Chelsea Bdg Rd Only' from which point it will doubtless return light to its depot. The date is alleged to be 6th October although if this is true the roadside trees seem to have shed their leaves remarkably early. Behind an RT works Route 186, one of the comparatively few to have run through this popular terminal point. (W.R.Legg)

Making its way on Route 3 to Hove Station, ex-B18 travels through Whitehawk on 20th January complete with its new ECW body, which had been fitted in March 1955. The chassis, a Bristol K6A fitted with the AEC 7.7 litre engine, originally carried a Duple utility body of relaxed design and had entered service in January 1946 with LPTB. Brighton, Hove & District acquired four of the batch which had comprised B10 to B29 and all were rebodied effectively extending their passenger use with this operator until all were disposed of in August 1965. (A.R.Packer)

Former D73, in common with the hundred of the class acquired by Belfast Corporation, received new Harkness bodywork of pleasing appearance during 1954 or 1955. Originally fitted with Brush utility bodywork for 56 passengers, this Daimler CWA6 had first entered Central Area service in June 1945, being garaged at Merton. Late in 1948 it received Green Line livery and joined other members of the class working the East End Green Line routes. In 1951 new RTs replaced these vehicles and they were all repainted for Central Area duties. Withdrawn from service and disposed of to W.North and Sons in January 1954 this bus was to last in passenger service until November 1970 with the Corporation.

In its operator's livery of blue and orange, ex-STL808 is now used on contract work with Smith's Luxury Coaches of Reading. Acquired from the same source as RT3 shown earlier in this book, the STL's life expectancy was much shorter and it was withdrawn and disposed of in November 1958. Initially the bus had entered service with London Transport in July 1935 from Dalston garage and ended its life in the capital garaged at Stockwell in October 1953. No alterations whatsoever have been made externally to the LPTB built body except for the livery change. (A.R.Packer)

Red liveried RT153 had been transferred into the Country Area Hitchin garage in December 1956 and was used there in passenger service for nearly a year before returning to Central bus duties. It is seen on January 19th in use on Route 801A at The White Lion Hotel in the High Street at Stevenage working one of the Tuesday and Saturday journeys to Hitchin. At this time the 801A was the main service from Longmeadow to Stevenage Station while the plain 801 was only a peak hour service from Shephall. This was to change in October of the year under review when the 801A number disappeared in favour of a revised 801 and 811, the latter operating the Tuesday and Saturday journeys non-stop between Stevenage and Hitchin. (A.R.Packer)

RT1121 is seen on 5th April at the Well Hall Station terminus in company with RF500. Route 182 was the replacement in the final stage of the tram conversion programme for Tram 46. The route operated between Cannon Street and Woolwich in its fullest extent but in this view the bus is in use on a short working. The experimental three line via point blind introduced on these routes in 1952 is still in use on this vehicle. (W.R.Legg)

RT1012 stands in Cecil Road, Enfield on 13th April before working back to Hertford garage at Fairfax Road. This is probably at the end of the peak period although the timetable for this date shows most such journeys working through to Hertford Bus Station before running in. This RT ran from Hertford from the summer of 1956 until July 1961. (W.R.Legg)

RM1 and RM2 originally had only one small destination aperture at the front and rear with a single line box above the rear platform, all in the cause of weight reduction. Neither bus saw passenger service with this configuration, both being remodelled and fitted with more conventional boxes. This rear view of RM2 at Kingston Station on Route 406A demonstrates the now standard appearance of the bus.

Transport enthusiasts, especially the longer serving members of LOTS, will recognise this particular registration immediately as belonging to RT1431 once owned by that society from February 1966 until moving on within the preservation movement. Starting its passenger service in May 1949 at Nunhead it was also to see service at Uxbridge, Middle Row and Stockwell before being taken out of service and stored at the last mentioned location in August 1955 until eventual disposal in April 1956. Bird's Commercial Motors handled all the Craven bodied RT disposals and many made the journey north with the A1 Service consortium purchasing twenty four initially. Just two of these 3RT3/4 are known to survive into 1998 as a reminder of the unique five bay constructed bodies built by Cravens for the RT family.

The later STLs were not a type of bus which frequented Potters Bar garage. However in 1953 STL1437 spent a short time at the most northerly Central Area garage. Here it crosses St.Giles' Circus on a journey which will terminate at Muswell Hill, Hampden Road. In 1953 several STLs were given back full blind displays, which considerably enhanced their appearance and this vehicle wears its seventeen years extremely well. (R.Wellings)

Its stint at Potters Bar finished, STL1437 moved across to Harrow Weald. The need for a full set of blinds seems to have proved to be something of a problem for the garage staff and a side or rear blind is fitted in the via points box. Route 209 was a service which had been introduced in May 1952 using STLs running through several previously unserved roads. After still further service at Upton Park garage in the first month of 1954 the bus was finally withdrawn and sent for scrap by Norths. (R.Wellings)

Three 'leaning back' STLs including STL404 and STL412, operate on private hire duties in the year of the Coronation. The two identifiable examples at least were disposed of before the year ended and this further work for them only extended over the celebration period. All three had entered service in 1934 fitted with petrol engines removed from LT class vehicles and these were replaced in 1939 by diesel units. (J.H.Aston)

The once bold new experimental Q1, with engine mounted to the offside side member behind the front wheels, now nears the end of its life in the role of a chicken house. In 1932 when the vehicle first entered service with the LGOC, it seated 37 passengers, was fitted with a bumper bar assembly, vertical sliding wiper blades and higher mounted headlamps. The front end was rebuilt during the vehicle's Country Area usage to closely resemble the 102 buses then being delivered in the second half of 1936 for use on Country bus services. Disposed of to a dealer in March 1946, it was to be used in passenger service for a further five years with C.J.Towler Ltd. of Emneth near Wisbech, Norfolk, before its humiliating final use for the benefit of poultry. (C.Bull collection)

Three AEC Regents look forlorn as they stand within the Dover Docks complex in 1953. From left to right are LPTB bodied STL1758 and STL409 and then Weymann bodied A42 formerly of the Liverpool Corporation Transport. STL409 was later exported while the other ex-London vehicle saw further use with a home based contractor but not the owner's of the antiquated concrete mixer. (R.F.Mack)

At least one house in the background shows patriotic fervour as STL2013 rests from its unaccustomed long journey while in use as a Green Line relief on service 710 to Central London on Coronation Day. 'To and From Coronation Terminals' notices are carried beneath the canopy and in the window adjacent to the rear platform. This 4/9STL14 had been one of a large number of the class to be retained for the Coronation special services and given an overhaul earlier in the year. Having completed its task it was immediately demoted to staff bus duties, in which capacity it lasted until July1955 when it was finally withdrawn. (A.M.Wright)

STL1455 was garaged at Alperton for the last year of its passenger use within the capital. With a full set of route blinds it journeys to Colindale Station on Route 79 wearing the latest colour scheme which it received at its last overhaul in April 1952. Originally entering service in July 1936 as a 3/9STL11, it carried body number 16469, this being exchanged for 16471 upon its March 1938 overhaul which was retained throughout the rest of its existence thereby keeping its same classification. It had worn Central Area livery since new until in December 1951 when it received Country Area colours but only until April 1952 when it reverted to red. Perhaps the Country Area did not appreciate the idea of using such an elderly bus. W.North of Leeds scrapped the vehicle in January 1954. (R.Wellings)

RLH73 stands within the clearly defined terminus area outside Morden Underground station waiting to depart for South Wimbledon Station by way of Route 127. The bus will negotiate a U turn to travel on a horseshoe shaped route to reach its destination which is a mile away using around ten miles of road. Many changes have taken place over the years to this corner of London Road and a comparison photograph today would reveal a huge office building as a background while in the foreground the road has taken much of the buses only area. (M.Rooum)

Before the end of 1953 T610, built in 1938 and initially entering service as a Green Line coach had been withdrawn from service eventually to be disposed of in the following year. Standing at Dorking North Station and now confined to bus duties it still carries its former Green Line colours but with London Transport fleetnames. It waits to depart for Guildford, Farnham Road with running plates GF3. Unlike many of its sisters, this particular vehicles spent the years of the Second World War in normal service, first at Epping and then Grays and escaped the indignities of ambulance or 'Clubmobile' service. (K.Lane)

With the opening of the new garage at North Street, Romford in August 1953, ten SRT class buses were included in the initial allocation, having been transferred from Barking, Forest Gate and Hornchurch and intended for the 66, 66A routes. SRT125, whose short career had involved operation at Twickenham, Cricklewood and Hornchurch has strayed on to Route 123 which in 1953 ran between Ongar and South Hornchurch. This particular SRT utilised the chassis of former STL2643 while the body, after a repaint into Green Line livery and fitting of side mounted totems between decks, next saw service as RT4489. (R.Wellings)

T779 journeys to Apsley Mills from Harpenden on Route 307A traversing minor country roads that appear to need attention from the ravages of the earlier winter months. This route originated in 1935 when the Apsley Mills journeys on 307 were renumbered 379. Then in 1941 the 379 number was replaced by the more logical 307A, which continued until May 1976 when the difficulties of three track number blinds saw the Apsley journeys revert to plain 307 first carried in 1933 thereby restoring the pre-1935 situation. (R.Wellings)

On 6th June 1953 at the Epsom Derby race meeting at least three different classes of bus will be transporting the immediate passengers to Morden Station on the special service provided. The lead bus, SRT137, will be followed by an STL and behind that a post-war STD. The SRT spent practically all its life garaged at Twickenham for use on Routes 90 and 90B and it was only in its last four months that it moved to Cricklewood for use on Route 16. (A.B.Cross)

This is one of those confusing pictures caused by the driver's inability to select the correct blind display. This is Station Road, Cuffley and TF31 is heading for Newgate Street and Hertford on Route 308, not 308A, although all the points shown on the blind will be served. Originally entering service as a Green Line coach in May 1939 and used as an ambulance during World War II, the coach returned to its former role in March 1946. Now in 1953 the vehicle is demoted to bus duties for its last few months of passenger use with London Transport. (R.Wellings)

RT496 is on temporary loan to Chalk Farm garage from Middle Row and a side/rear blind has been hurriedly fitted giving a double exposure of the route number. Outshopped from its May 1952 overhaul in the latest livery, the bus otherwise reflects its original condition. For the car enthusiast a lovely Armstrong Siddeley Lancaster saloon first registered in December 1950 follows the bus through the road junction at Camden Town. (P.J.Marshall)

STL1741 ended its career with London Transport allocated to Grays from October 1953 until delicensed in September 1954. Here it waits in Clarence Road, Grays before running a works journey on the 380 to the Bata Shoe Factory via East Tilbury. (R.Wellings)

Ray Stenning in an article in the 'London Bus Magazine' in 1977 described the routes around Oxted as 'The Puppy Bus'. Here are a couple of the puppies - a year or so previous they would have been cubs - intent it would seem on going together to Holland. Both GS1 and GS14 had entered service at Chelsham in October 1953 and both are now preserved. In this early stage of their lives, trafficators and grab handles below the windscreen have yet to be added. Of particular interest is the diminutive bus stop flag fitted to a cast iron post, which was standard in the Country Area at one time. (R.Wellings)

Single deck TD52 is sandwiched between RT2726 and trolleybus 128 in this scene taken at Edgware garage yard during February 1954. The trolleybus dating from December 1935 is now withdrawn from passenger use and waits movement to Cardiff for scrapping. The TD, new in December 1948, lasted in passenger service within the capital until withdrawn in November 1958 after which it found further use with the Ceylon Transport Board. It was not until May 1975 that the RT finally left London having initially entered service in December 1951. (K.Lane)

Only three overhead wire lubricator vehicles were ever owned by London Transport. The first was numbered 41H and used the chassis of NS760 being in use from November 1936 until destroyed in October 1940. The second, 114W, is seen here in the Old Kent Road, rather distant from any overhead wiring and without the lubricator heads fitted to the poles. It was rebuilt in 1938 from the chassis of T320, which was once fitted with a Hall Lewis coach body seating 29 passengers. The service vehicle remained in use until June 1957 when it was delicensed and put in store at Lea Bridge trolleybus depot before being moved to Chiswick for eventual sale in May 1959. The third vehicle was 734J and utilised the chassis of STL12, being withdrawn in March 1955. (M.Rooum)

STL2117 resided at Sidcup garage during the first few months of 1954 before transfer to Merton and immediate withdrawal from passenger use in April. In July 1937, when the bus first entered service, it carried a Park Royal metal framed body number 17538, to be outshopped from its first overhaul with an identical body numbered 17551. Suffering from acute corrosion the body was removed in May 1949 and replaced with an LPTB 1939 composite built example numbered 121, which had previously graced the chassis of STL2589. Now in its last period of passenger operation it is seen at Orpington waiting to depart for Bexleyheath Depot by way of Route 229. RT3436, parked further in the distance, is just two years into its life with London Transport that ended in 1971. (M.Rooum)

At the Uxbridge terminus RF610 waits departure on Route 459 to the Richings Park Estate situated beside Iver railway station. All the Country Area bus variants of the RF class entered service in 1953 and Windsor garage received their initial intake during the early summers months with this particular bus not transferring further afield until November 1957 when it moved to Hertford. (A.Mortimer)

New as a Green Line coach in May 1938 allocated to Staines garage, T489 spent the war years as an ambulance and returned to Green Line work at Amersham in March 1946. In 1951 it became one of the forty such vehicles modified for use as Central Area buses and saw service from Kingston and Leyton garages. Disposed of to W.North of Leeds in August 1953 it had found its way by 29th August 1955 to Belgrade, Yugoslavia where it is seen in the Place Republik carrying registration plate C2440 and fleet number 91 although the name of the owner is not known. A rather clever piece of rebuilding has provided it with an offside passenger saloon doorway (J.C.Gillham)

GS82, delivered to London Transport in January 1954, was stored at Garston and later Reigate before eventually being found work in December at Crawley garage together with GS81 and GS83 which, up to this time, had a parallel history. The background to this view is typical of the operational environment found on new routes 852 and 852A, which had replaced the Hants & Sussex operation in December 1954. In May 1955 the services were cut back from Ewhurst to only operate as far as Horsham.

Former STD72 is seen while in the ownership of Hutfield's Coaches (Warwick) Ltd. with a solitary one line of route information showing 'Coventry'. The nameplate fixed to the top of the radiator carries its operator's name, while a driver's cab door of dubious quality has been fitted. After further owners this all Leyland product was last documented as parked on the premises of Young's International Cars Ltd. of Grays in April 1958 and one is left with a question mark as to its final fate. (D.A.Jones)

D203 can be seen in the 1953 book of this series when in the ownership of London Transport but now it operates with the South Western Omnibus Company of Colombo, Ceylon. The bus has undergone superficial changes to the exterior with rebuilt front route box and a flat panel in place of the blind box above the rear platform. Note the bus stop sign with the quaint wording 'MOTOR BUS HALTING PLACE' which somehow sounds more polite than 'BUS STOP'! (A.B.Cross)

This full fronted highbridge Duple Midland (Nudd) bodied bus with seating for 55 and Scottish registration hides the fact that it is carried on a modified chassis which earlier had been London Transport G173 with NCME 56 seat bodywork incorporating austerity features. The bus first entered service in July 1945 at Victoria, primarily for working Routes 52 and 77A, but the entire garage complement of Guys were transferred to Enfield in November. In February 1952 this particular bus was withdrawn and purchased by Edinburgh Corporation who acquired sixty examples in total. All were rebodied before entering service in their new environment and on 31st July 1955 ex-G173 is seen in Charlotte Square on Route 22 to Stonehouse. (F.Church)

After a career with London Transport spanning the years 1935 through to 1953, STL806 was to find further use as a mobile furniture showroom after disposal. G.Henster Ltd. of London, E9, manufacturers of Serenity chairs and Zenith furniture operated the vehicle in a dark red and grey livery from 1954 to 1959, after which it was disposed of to Sparks, a dealer of London SW2. With panelled over route box apertures, it is seen parked within the Cardiff Central bus station in July 1955. (A.R.Packer)

Norbiton's RT1745 works the Wimbledon tennis special service in 1955 to and from Southfields Station. The two termini are little under a mile apart but obviously the service provided a link much appreciated by the enthusiastic followers of the sport several of whom can be seen sprawled on the pavement, possibly after an all night vigil to gain early entry. Upon its next overhaul the bus returned to service with a roof route box type body, number 1673, which was to curtail its passenger use in London in May 1963.

Seen at the Western SMT premises in Carlisle on 30th July 1955, two rather different looking former London G class buses await their respective departure times. On the left ex-G47, originally fitted with Weymann bodywork, now carries a secondhand Croft lowbridge 55 seat body with fleet number DY1050 and appears to be about to leave for Longtown. On the right ex-G112 had its Park Royal body replaced by a new Alexander lowbridge example and was given fleet number DY1001. With a healthy passenger load it will soon depart for Lockerbie, the longer of the two routes ending in a town which is now synonymous with terrorist disasters. (F.Church)

A.G.Lindfield, growers of Thakeham, Sussex acquired six C type buses in 1955 for use with the transport of workers involved in their industry. C4, 36, 50, 53, 90 and 98 received fleet numbers 1, 6, 5, 4, 3 and 2 respectively. Ex-C50, parked on typical farmland with the South Downs rising in the distance, waits further use at the end of the day. All six passed to Voakes, a dealer of nearby Billinghurst, in the summer of 1962 having been a familiar sight for seven years on the roads around Thakeham. (Surfleet Transport Photographs)

RT4801 is seen at the Leatherhead terminus of Route 65 with destination blind already set for a journey to Ealing, Argyle Road, the furthermost terminus of the service. A short career of less than ten years with London Transport was the result of an overhaul in June 1957 when the bus was outshopped with body number 1530, which had originally graced the chassis of RT281 of 1948 vintage. Having first entered service in February 1954 from Twickenham it was transferred to its current garage, Norbiton, in August 1955. Until 1979 it was the highest numbered RT to have been disposed of and caused some surprise when it entered service with H & C Transport of Garston in March 1963. (A.Mortimer)

Passengers board GS81 on Route 852 at 'The George', Crawley in December 1956 before its driver has had time to reset the blind to Horsham. This scene is far removed from the atmosphere of the New Town which was growing up all around. The yard to the right, which once echoed to hooves of horses bringing carriages in and the well constructed bus shelter on the left have an air of timelessness which alas may soon be shattered. (A.R.Packer)

At the end of its journey from Kingston, T785 is seen beside an awkwardly placed alighting point in Staines. The driver appears concerned with the jay walking activities of the children beside the bus and seems to be remonstrating with the adult in charge. The bus had been transferred to the Central Area in August 1956 to operate from Kingston garage. (A.Mortimer)

This sparse bus station at King Street, East Grinstead is now a car park in which places have to be queued for and cars inched into position such is the demand. In 1956 car ownership was yet to threaten the existence of the delightfully rural 494 service to Oxted, which had been introduced in 1948 and the steamy windows of GS59 suggest it has been well patronised. (A.R.Packer)

During the period March 1956 through to March 1960 RT3611 carried the Weymann body number 2246, which had been mounted on the chassis of RT967 when new. Throughout this period it was allocated to Two Waters garage and in the summer of 1956 it is seen at Hemel Hempstead bus station waiting departure for St.Albans on Route 314. With the winter programme of route changes, the 314 was withdrawn on 16th October, being replaced by the extension of Route 330. Oddly the 314A, a Hemel Hempstead town service, continued to exist for some time. (R.Wellings)

On 23rd July the British Road Services' yard in Dock Street, Dundee provides temporary refuge for a number of RTs including, in the front row left to right, RTs1433, 1423 and 1421, which were to enter service with the Corporation Transport Department as their fleet numbers 224, 228 and 234 respectively later in the year. All were to serve their new owners until 1968, which was some considerable number of years more than were spent in London passenger use. The left hand example is in red livery while the other two are in Country Area green and except for the removal of the route blinds are in 'as withdrawn' condition. (A.R.Packer)

The 'pre-war' RTs allocated to Hertford to cover Route 327, which had a weight restriction, occasionally wandered elsewhere on the garage's routes. Here RT62 runs alongside the New River at Ware on Route 350A to Bishops Stortford, Havers Lane Estate.

T787 is seen at Crawley in December 1956 operating a short journey to Horley on Route 405, the trunk West Croydon to Horsham service normally operated with double deck buses. The bus has resided at this southern Country Area garage since August 1953 when it re-entered service from its July overhaul but now it carries evidence of the wintry condition of the roads. (A.R.Packer)

In the early part of the year RT1515 is seen in its last throes of passenger use with London Transport at Purley while in use on route 190 which was operated by Thornton Heath garage. Before the year-end it was in service with Dundee Corporation Transport as their fleet number 237. It was to spend a greater number of years in passenger service in the north than it did in London. In its short number of years with the Executive it had seen service from Cricklewood, Catford, Holloway, Forest Gate, Leyton and lastly Thornton Heath. (A.Mortimer)

Dundee Corporation Transport replaced its trams with buses between November 1955 and October 1956. To expedite their demise ten Weymann bodied 18STL20s were purchased from London in 1955 followed by thirty Craven bodied RTs in 1956. Ex-STL2688 is seen in the city centre operating as a duplicate on Route 21 to Balgay Road, once served by electric traction. Having received a repaint into Corporation green and white and unmarred by any advertising, the bus contrasts greatly with the following tram. The GPO used Morris Commercial vans in great numbers and one of these is seen parked outside the local branch of Burton tailoring. (F.W.Ivey)

APPENDIX I

London Transport Central and Country Area Bus Garages

Code	Garage	Code	Garage
A	Sutton	K	Kingston
AB	Twickenham	L	Loughton
AC	Willesden	LH*	Leatherhead
AD	Palmers Green	LS*	Luton
AE	Hendon	M	Mortlake
AF	Chelverton Road, Putney	MA*	Amersham
AK	Streatham	MH	Muswell Hill
AL	Merton	N	Norwood
AM	Plumstead	NB	Norbiton
AP	Seven Kings	NF*	Northfleet
AR	Tottenham	NS	North Street, Romford
AV	Hounslow	NX	New Cross
AW	Abbey Wood	ON	Alperton
B	Battersea	P	Old Kent Road
BK	Barking	PB	Potters Bar
BN	Brixton	PM	Peckham
C	Athol Street, Poplar	Q	Camberwell
CA	Clapham	R	Riverside
CF	Chalk Farm	RD	Hornchurch
CL	Clay Hall	RE*	London Road, Romford
CM*	Chelsham	RG*	Reigate
CS	Chiswick (non-operational)	RL	Rye Lane
CY*	Crawley	S	Shepherds Bush
D	Dalston	SA*	St.Albans
DG*	Dunton Green	SJ*	Swanley Junction
DS*	Dorking	SP	Sidcup
DT*	Dartford	ST*	Staines
E	Enfield	SV*	Stevenage
ED	Elmers End	SW	Stockwell
EG*	East Grinstead	T	Leyton
EP*	Epping	TB	Bromley
EW	Edgware	TC	Croydon
F	Putney Bridge	TG*	Tring
G	Forest Gate	TH	Thornton Heath
GD*	Godstone	TL	Catford
GF*	Guildford	TW*	Tunbridge Wells
GM	Gillingham Street, Victoria	U	Upton Park
GR*	Garston	UX	Uxbridge
GY*	Grays	V	Turnham Green
H	Hackney	W	Cricklewood
HD	Harrow Weald	WA*	Watford High Street
HE*	High Wycombe	WD	Wandsworth
HF*	Hatfield	WG	West Green
HG*	Hertford	WL	Walworth
HH*	Two Waters	WR*	Windsor
HN*	Hitchin	WY*	Addlestone
HW	Southall	X	Middle Row
J	Holloway	-	Aldenham (non-operational)

* indicates a Country Area garage.

In 1957 no new garages were brought into use and none were found to be surplus to requirements. However, the on-going programme to modernise existing premises continued.

APPENDIX II

I have continued to receive many helpful letters adding or correcting the information in previous volumes in this series. Among those writing since the publication of the last title have been J.M.Burrows, Nicholas King, Roger Whitehead and Alan Wood. Special thanks are extended to Barry Maynard-Smith who provides extensive information regarding the private cars that appear in many of the photographs. Although the books are about buses and coaches it is evident from correspondence received that many readers are appreciative of this ancillary service. Please continue to write if you can add further information or you spot an error. The team who compile the captions are not infallible and welcome these corrections.

The following added information is therefore provided for previously published books in the series:

GENERAL

It has been pointed out that the term 'duty number' has been incorrectly used a number of times in previous books. To clarify and correct: the plates carried by a bus (e.g. UX 3 or BN 7) are 'running numbers' referring to the schedule being performed by the bus on that route on that day. 'Duty numbers' are the numbers or rosters allocated to the crews operating the buses. Several duty numbers will be involved in working a running number during the day.

I hope that has made it clear but it is an interesting point that Centrewest Buses at least now use a system whereby the number displayed on the bus is actually the duty number of the driver or crew operating the bus! The theory behind the introduction of this system was that when there were service delays it avoided several crews waiting at changeover points for their bus to turn up - instead they take over the next one that comes along.

1962 BOOK

Page 24 The car referred to in the bottom picture is a Ford Prefect 105E first registered in April 1961 and not a Ford Popular as stated.

Page 37 The top picture is taken in High Street, Harpenden.

Page 66 A bull nosed Morris car stands behind the Q in Tottenham garage.

Page 96 The car in the top picture is a Vauxhall Mark I Victor and not a Viva as stated.

Page 102 RT686 is traversing Clarence Street, Kingston.

Page 107 The device fitted to RT4725 for measuring numbers of passengers was called a loadmeter, not a loadmaster.